Building
PEOPLE

SOCIAL-EMOTIONAL LEARNING
FOR KIDS, FAMILIES, SCHOOLS & COMMUNITIES

EDITED BY TAMARA FYKE

Building
PEOPLE

SOCIAL-EMOTIONAL LEARNING
FOR KIDS, FAMILIES, SCHOOLS & COMMUNITIES

Abingdon Press™

Nashville

BUILDING PEOPLE: SOCIAL-EMOTIONAL LEARNING
FOR KIDS, FAMILIES, SCHOOLS & COMMUNITIES

This book is printed on acid-free paper.

Library of Congress Cataloging-in-Publication Data has been requested.

ISBN: 978-1-5018-7800-8

18 19 20 21 22 23 24 25 26 27—10 9 8 7 6 5 4 3 2 1
MANUFACTURED IN THE UNITED STATES OF AMERICA

CONTENTS

Rod Berger

FOREWORD: BUILDING PEOPLE TAKES A VILLAGE

Dr. Rod Berger is President and CEO of MindRocket Media Group and works on strategy and communications with education companies worldwide. A former school administrator and an education technology leader, he has had his work featured in *Forbes* and *Huffington Post*, hosted panel discussions at leading education conferences, and developed content and presentations that have driven successful strategies for some of the most prominent companies in education and edtech.

One of the many privileges of my role in education is that I get to interact with leaders and stakeholders nationally and, in fact, globally. I work with leaders from every background whose positions in the industry take every shape and form. From teachers to superintendents, community advocates to policymakers, and edtech startup founders to some of the biggest names in international education, I have the chance to see, hear, and absorb the perspectives and experiences of the people who are making a difference for students in every way possible.

Over the past decade-plus, one of the most encouraging developments I've witnessed is the onward march of social-emotional learning (SEL). While there have been researchers and practitioners focusing on SEL for at least 25 years, it wasn't long ago that the topic was mostly relegated to the fringes of the education conversation. It wasn't a "core" academic subject and wasn't a part of education policy, so it was an "extra." We wanted kids to grow up emotionally healthy and have a well-rounded set of competencies, but there wasn't consensus buy-in that schools were *really* responsible for making it happen.

That has changed in a major way. While there's still an implementation gap where states, districts, schools, and classrooms haven't all collectively made plans for intentional SEL, the education community has made huge strides forward in understanding the urgency and high priority of including support and instruction on matters that are "nonacademic." Almost all educators now will say that SEL is important, and plenty of organizations have the research and strategies to prove that it is practical and can be done. Social-emotional learning helps students perform better academically and prepares them for success in the real world. Now we are in the ever-important home stretch: making it a reality for all learners.

In this book, some common themes emerge. There are many leaders, in different contexts, who were doing social-emotional learning before it had a proper name. In the mid-1990s, with pioneering research demonstrating SEL's importance and the founding of the Collaborative for Academic, Social, and Emotional Learning (CASEL), progress toward real implementation began to accelerate. Still, though, many educators feel underprepared to take a lead role in facilitating kids' social-emotional development. Especially with increased stress, anxiety, and trauma—often hidden beneath the surface—affecting a higher percentage of the kids in our classrooms and communities, adults need help identifying and addressing social-emotional and mental health needs. To do this right, voices from all corners must be—and increasingly have been—amplified. SEL is an *everybody* thing. Student, teacher, and parent. Administrator, advocate, and community leader. Everyone must contribute to these efforts. Strong SEL can't afford a weak link, and there's major opportunity lost when anyone's ideas are left out.

What excites me most about this book is that it brings together contributors whose expertise and achievements in advancing SEL are as diverse as they are impressive. Their unique perspectives give us the opportunity to truly look at the project of "building people" from all angles. Whatever your personal experience with SEL—whether you've been promoting it as an educator for decades, doing so at home or in the community without even realizing it, or giving it thought for the first time—you'll find multiple new ways of looking at pressing SEL issues and thinking through solutions.

Building People presents perspectives that can meet you wherever your current challenges lie. It's designed not only to be read, but also to be revisited and referenced. It's a volume packed with big names and big ideas, but its concepts are relatable, reliable, and easy to digest. From my own perspective, I'm encouraged by the current state of SEL and excited for the future. This isn't to get too far ahead of ourselves. The opportunity cost if we don't universally commit to intentional SEL is still huge. If we miss one child, that's one too many, and we're not yet close to reaching them all. However, I've observed this opinion becoming commonplace. Belief is the first step to making an initiative stick, and educators *do believe.*

This book isn't the end of our SEL journey. Depending on where you currently are, it may not be your beginning. But for all of us who believe in equitable educational outcomes, this collaborative and communicative process is one we must engage in. This is where we model exactly what we want from our learners: hear from diverse perspectives, consider new ideas, and synthesize it all into a new plan of action. Whatever your next step may be, I'm glad we're on this journey together.

Tamara Fyke

HOW ALL EDUCATION STAKEHOLDERS CAN MAKE SEL A PRIORITY

Tamara Fyke is a creative entrepreneur with a passion for kids, families, and urban communities, and is the creator, author, and brand manager for Love In A Big World.[1] Tamara received her master's degree in education from Vanderbilt University's Peabody College of Education and Human Development and worked at Vanderbilt's Center for Safe & Supportive Schools providing professional development, coaching, and consulting for principals and teachers for issues related to safety and climate.

I. CURRENT STATE OF SEL

For centuries, social-emotional learning (SEL) has been woven into the fabric of education. Great minds, from Aristotle to Franklin to King, have defined education as more than facts and figures; it is about the personal development of body, mind, and spirit. When I started my work in education in 1996, educators and community leaders were focused on what was then known as character education and presently would be referred to as SEL. Many education and community leaders were working to make this a focus of our national educational agenda. The federal Office of Safe and Drug-Free Schools was fully funded and allocated some dollars to character initiatives.[2] However, at that time, there was not much research around the impact of SEL on students, teachers, and the school community.

From 2003 to 2007, I had the privilege of being part of one of the first federal research projects related to SEL with the U.S. Department of Education, Mathematica, and Vanderbilt University, called the Social and Character Development Research Program (SACD). The work of the organization I founded, including its curriculum, was being evaluated. Our principal investigator, Dr. Leonard Bickman, drew upon the work of Hawkins and Catalano with the Communities That Care model and Bandura's self-efficacy theory.[3-4] I have two big takeaways from this five-year project. For any school-wide initiative to be impactful, there must be strong principal leadership. Likewise, effective program implementation requires teacher buy-in, and teacher buy-in is in direct correlation to principal leadership.

Once No Child Left Behind became law in 2002, the emphasis in education became data and evaluation.[5] Coupled with focus on test scores was the reallocation of funding from programs like the state grants provided by Safe and Drug-Free Schools and Communities to the wars in the Middle East.[6] Data and evaluation are important but only to the degree that they are used in service of the student. Fast forward fifteen years, and we now see the pendulum swinging, hopefully to a place of balance. With the talk about adverse childhood experiences (ACEs) and trauma-informed practice, we are seeing educators and community leaders wake up to the fact that children are more than numbers. They are people.

It's an exciting time to be part of education, especially as related to social-emotional learning. There is a growing awareness among global and local leaders that we must attend to the needs of the whole child. Not only do we have superintendents and principals championing the cause, but we also have teachers who are dedicated to what is best for children.

II. Cost of Maintaining the Status Quo

A few years ago, when I worked at the Center for Safe and Supportive Schools at Vanderbilt, I heard Tim Shriver speak about his work with the

Collaborative for Academic, Social, and Emotional Learning (CASEL).[7-8] He showed us two images that articulated the way that I have thought about character education and SEL for many years. Every initiative that we undertake at a school—whether it is violence prevention, school-family-community partnerships, substance abuse prevention, health and sex education, academic intervention, or drop-out prevention—is related to SEL. What is needed is a common framework—a common language. The first image below shows all the programs a school may be implementing without any over-arching framework; the second image illustrates how all of these initiatives can be organized and made cohesive within the framework of SEL.

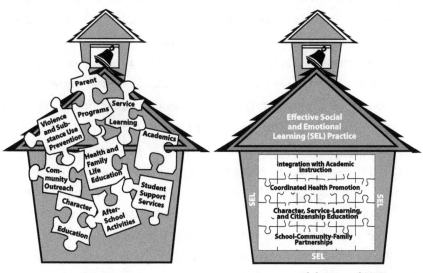

Images provided courtesy of CASEL

What I see as the cost of maintaining the status quo is that we will have a lot of time and money spent on professional development, research, and lip service for SEL without making a measurable change where it matters most—with our kids.

Real change requires a comprehensive overhaul to the way we do school. If we are not careful, we will jump on the bandwagon of SEL and tout our programs rather than build relationships. Relationships change people, not programs. Building relationships requires time and conversation. In order to connect with one another, we must speak the same language.

III. FORECAST FOR THE FUTURE

SEL Strategy

When I look at the future of SEL, I see a need for a universal prevention strategy within individual schools and organizations as well as across the ecosystem of children's lives. In order for us to make real progress in policy and practice, leaders from all sectors of society must come together and voice the need. Although SEL has been mandated in many states, it has not been funded to the extent necessary to support the work of the teachers, school counselors, and social workers who are working with students day in and day out.

There are caring adults serving our schools and communities who want to be part of positive change for students and provide the first line of defense in order to stop problems before they start. What they need is content for meaningful conversations. Many schools have time allotted for morning meetings or advisory periods, but with the rigors of teaching academics, teachers do not have the time to create SEL lesson plans or coordinate efforts across the school community so that everyone is speaking the same language.

When I'm leading professional development with teachers, I tell them, "Whether you are aware of it or not, you are already teaching SEL. What we want to do is provide a common language for you and your students so you can be more intentional with your SEL practice." This intentionality causes us to seize the teachable moments that occur as we are walking down the hallway, standing at the water fountain, or outside playing at recess. Additionally, an integration of SEL with academics helps make the academic subject area more relevant and more human. It helps students see how they can use what they're learning as part of their real world experience.

The focus is on building relationships: teacher-student, student-student, and teacher-teacher. Granting teachers time to focus on relationships will help them and their students thrive because we are creating a place where people are acknowledged and valued for who they are, not just what they do. This sounds simple, but it is not always easy. It means saying hello to people, sharing a smile, noticing when someone has a bad day, and having conversations about difficult things with the goal of coming to greater understanding of one another. With a united focus on universal prevention, resources can be targeted for specific interventions for students dealing with higher levels of trauma.

Evaluation, Data, and Iteration

Part of the work with which I am currently involved is helping schools and youth organizations refine their approaches to SEL evaluation. How do we show that students are learning these SEL competencies—that change is happening and healthy relationships are growing? Additionally, how do we find out where we as caring adults are missing the mark and can improve our approach? We have to include evaluation as part of our SEL work.

The challenge is that SEL can be difficult to measure—that's what we found with the SACD project. However, we can collect a lot of qualitative data and anecdotal evidence related to impact. In addition to specific SEL measures that are competency focused, we can utilize measures related to school culture and climate. Culture is what we do; climate is how it feels. Long term, we can look at academic, behavioral, and health gains; short term, we can look at engagement. Are the methods we are using to teach SEL meaningful and relevant to kids?

We must pair the qualitative and the quantitative. The data tells us what is working and what is not working. Just because SEL cannot be measured in the same way as mathematics or reading skills does not mean it cannot be measured. It means it is a challenge to measure. This is where both the evaluation and practice of SEL have room to iterate. Again, we must be mindful of our purpose—cultivating relationships and building people.

IV. Pathway to Success

To ensure the success of the SEL movement, educationally sound and commercially viable content and tools are needed.

Educationally sound

What we do in the field of SEL must be grounded in research. Both the content and the process need to align with educational theory. Even though SEL itself is difficult to measure, we can provide SEL instruction using proven methods for teaching and learning. Utilizing an interdisciplinary approach that incorporates literacy, arts, and service, as well as conversation, rest, and play, assures that we are meeting the needs of the whole child. The work I do is built on Piaget, Vygotsky, Freire, Bandura, Hawkins, Catalano, and others in the field of education and positive youth development. This approach gives space for student voice, which lets students know that they are valued.

Commercially viable

If we are going to obtain and sustain the attention of students in our media-saturated world, we must meet them with content that is attractive and compelling. It must look and feel kid-friendly and fun. Not only must the content look relevant, it must be substantive. Students as young as six years old are capable of having conversations about important issues, such as race and bullying. They have an amazing capacity for understanding the big issues and developing practical solutions for our world. We don't need to talk down to them. Instead, we need to facilitate meaningful conversations, coach them when they are struggling, and learn along with them.

When I was a kid, there were TV shows like *ABC Afterschool Special* during the week and *Schoolhouse Rock* on Saturday mornings. There were kid-friendly PSA announcements running as regular commercials. There was a lot of media attention around positive youth development. I think we've lost that type of TV programming. It's been replaced with popular talk shows and other media, and I believe we are missing a common branding where people can circle around and say, "This is what we want to promote as becoming a better person," or "This is what it means to build our community."

I think there's an opportunity for those of us in education and other sectors of our society to come together so that we're meeting kids across the ec system. Whether that's school, healthcare, entertainment, or business, it's a way for us to coalesce. There have been attempts. However, although these initiatives provided a framework for people and a way that they could talk about SEL as adults, they didn't provide the hands-on activities for kids. I think it's important to provide practical tools for caring adults. By and large, the people that I talk to say, "Hey, this stuff is really important. I wish I had this when I was a kid. What can I do?" They need a toolbox.

Changing the Climate

Many people in our world are living in fear of the next mass shooting or natural disaster. It is our job as educators and community leaders to transform the climate from fear to love. SEL helps us identify what is going on in our heads and in our hearts so we use our hands to build up and not tear down.

There's a river running through our society that, unfortunately, focuses on the negative and tends to ignore the positive. It's important to not always focus on the negative but instead turn our attention to the positive and look at the kinds of things kids are doing from a positive youth development standpoint to make a difference in the world. From a theoretical standpoint, it's positive reinforcement. Let's look at the good and reinforce that from a positive perspective. If we're continually putting forward bullying, what are we going to see? More bullying! If we're putting forward more of the positive, then we're going to change the social norm. Let's look at student volunteer hours. Let's look at their maker projects, including youth entrepreneurship and the arts, and see how kids are contributing. By doing so, we lift everyone up.

When we commit, as both caring adults and youth, to a lifestyle of building up and not tearing down, then we are producing a safe place for everyone to learn and grow. We are providing a place for people to belong. We are creating family.

Editor's Reflection Questions

- What SEL strategies do you have that are focused on prevention? What SEL strategies do you have that are focused on intervention? What ties your prevention and intervention efforts together?
- What practical and hands-on tools for caring adults, including teachers, youth leaders, and families, do your SEL efforts have?
- How do you measure culture and climate?

NOTES

1. For more information about Love In A Big World, consult *LoveInABigWorld.org.* More information about Love In A Big World can also be found by connecting with me on LinkedIn and following *@entrprenurgirl* and *@loveinabigworld* on Twitter.

2. The Office of Safe and Drug-Free Schools is now defunct. For archived information about the program and its efforts, consult *www2.ed.gov/about/offices/list /osdfs/index.html.*

3. For more information about Communities That Care, consult *www .communitiesthatcare.net/about.*

4. Albert Bandura. "Self-Efficacy: Toward a Unifying Theory of Behavioral Change." *Psychological Review* 84, no. 2 (1977): 191-215.

5. For more information about No Child Left Behind, consult *https://www2.ed.gov /nclb/landing.jhtml.*

6. The annual funding appropriated for state grants from the federal Safe and Drug-Free Schools and Communities program was reduced by over 100 million dollars between 2003 and 2006. For more information about this program and its funding, consult "Safe and Drug-Free Schools and Communities: State Grants," U.S. Department of Education, last modified November 1, 2011, *https://www2 .ed.gov/programs/dvpformula/index.html.*

7. For more information about the Center for Safe and Supportive Schools, consult *https://my.vanderbilt.edu/tn-s3-center-vanderbilt/.*

8. For more information about the Collaborative for Academic, Social, and Emotional Learning, consult *casel.org.*

Maurice Elias

GUIDING RESEARCH-BASED PRACTICES INTO THE SEL 2.0 ERA

Maurice Elias, PhD, is Professor of Psychology at Rutgers University and the Director of the Rutgers Social-Emotional and Character Development Lab. He lectures internationally to educators and parents about students' emotional intelligence, school success, and social-emotional development. He is a founding member of the leadership team for the Collaborative for Academic, Social, and Emotional Learning.

I. ORIGINS OF SEL

Social-emotional learning (SEL) existed as a concept before it was defined and categorized as a practice. Back in graduate school in the mid-1970s, I came to see how important it was for children to have certain basic skills in school, like being able to pay attention, wait their turn, listen carefully, and possess the ability to deal with their own strong, emerging emotions. When I first started working in schools as an educational professional, it became very obvious to me that these were essential basic skills in the classroom.

In graduate school, my research showed that kids who lacked these basic skills were the kids usually labeled as having a "psychopathology," a diagnosis that followed them and negatively affected their entire educational experiences for the rest of their lives.[1] This was really cemented for me in my graduate school practicum with the Hartley-Salmon Child and Family Clinic in Hartford, Connecticut. As a practicum student, I was invisible to the staff. I would sit in the staff room and listen as people would complain, saying, "If only this would happen! If only that had happened! If only the school had done this or that!" And everything they were saying struck me as things that were entirely possible. The school could have been doing those things, and parents could have been doing these things, and the outcome would have been better if they did. But the structures to facilitate this communication and help those solutions happen systematically were either lacking or simply nonexistent. That was when I began to carve out my path forward in the social-emotional learning framework.

Social-emotional learning as a practice itself came about when Dan Goleman published his book *Emotional Intelligence* in 1995.[2] The book had chapters on applications of emotional intelligence in many different areas of society, and one of the chapters was focused on emotional intelligence in schools. Dan Goleman's book put the emotions where they belong—front and center—by drawing attention to various neuropsychological research showing how the emotional processes in the brain were, in fact, influencing the very same cognitive processes that we had been focusing on as educators. A passionate group of people, including Tim Shriver, Linda Lantieri, Mark Greenberg, and Roger Weissberg, began to talk about how to take this work in emotional intelligence and systematically apply it to the schools and the general education system.

This led to the formation of the organization named CASEL, which, at the time of its formation, stood for the Collaborative for the Advancement of Social and Emotional Learning.[3] A lot of debate went into that name, especially around whether "emotional" should be included in the organization's title. There was a vocal group that felt that mentioning emotions in the title would make schools not interested in the work of the organization. In the past, these things were thought of as social competence and social cognitive skills, with much less emphasis on the emotional part. Ultimately, though, the research won the day, and that is why we're talking about emotional processes here and now.

Social-emotional learning really became an official term in 1997 with the publication of *Promoting Social and Emotional Learning: Guidelines for*

Educators by ASCD (formerly known as the Association for Supervision and Curriculum Development).[4-5] That was a big step. Over 100,000 copies of the book were distributed, and people began to explore, define, and expand the field.

Interestingly enough, though, real traction for the theory and philosophy did not take place until CASEL changed its name. In 2001, a meeting of superintendents of schools and other district officials convened at the Fetzer Institute in Kalamazoo, Michigan, to discuss SEL and its lack of traction in classrooms and schools. The Fetzer Institute was founded by John Fetzer, a philanthropist and visionary who invented the lights that are used in night baseball and the unidimensional radio wave, which serves as the foundation of our system for radio stations. Later in his life, he turned his attention toward spirituality and health-related issues, including social-emotional life and well-being, so it's only fitting that the Fetzer Institute was the site of a major moment in the history of SEL.

At the Fetzer Institute retreat, we focused on the same question: "Social-emotional learning is a great thing, so why is it not getting traction?" It turned out the problem wasn't the inclusion of "emotional" in CASEL's name, as some suspected. The problem was the lack of the word "academic"—it gave teachers and administrators pause. So CASEL changed its name to the Collaborative for Academic, Social, and Emotional Learning, exchanging the word "academic" for the word "advancement" so that the name could change without changing the acronym. That change launched CASEL and the SEL field into the stratosphere. Mentioning "academic" acknowledged the main purpose of the practice for educators and really made a tremendous difference in the uptake and acceptance by educators across the country.

II. CURRENT STATE OF SEL

Almost every successful social-emotional program has a morning meeting, a sharing circle, or some other period of time when people get together and talk. The communication and common language used is very important for the successful implementation of a program.

There's also a societal perspective to examine regarding current issues of civil discourse. We're starting to see a growing recognition that social-emotional factors are critical elements of everyday life both inside and outside of the school. The general public doesn't universally understand this, but it is much more widely appreciated in education than it was three to five years ago. But even though it has become more appreciated and accepted, it doesn't automatically bring with it the organized and effective structure necessary to follow those beliefs.

A district is often going to have violence prevention programs, drug and opiate prevention programs, and special suicide prevention programs set up. All of these programs can be considered as efforts to address social-emotional issues, so when a school has a social-emotional curriculum or approach, they can handle conversations around every one of these issues without breaking stride because they have a language and a framework in place that they can use to talk about it. There is built-in social-emotional learning and character development. Whether we are talking about someone who makes a bad decision with drugs or guns or cheating or bullying, we're talking about a common set of skill deficiencies and character issues that are not separated out. The issue is that, when we start to define and compartmentalize different problem content areas, we draw a lot of attention away from the central issues. We distract kids, and we distract teachers. We drive everyone nuts.

When tragic events happen, we need to have the structures already in place and ready if we're ever going to be proactive and get past a reactive mode. If something terrible happens in the world, we want our kids to know about it, but currently we don't ask them to look at it in a familiar language. Instead, we teach them a new language to process the content. Metaphorically, it's like teaching them French and insisting they read an article about the shooting in Parkland, Florida, in French rather than in English. It's absurd to imagine us doing something like that, yet that's almost exactly what we do when traumatic and catastrophic social events happen.

On a national scene, we see tremendous public sentiment against guns, but it's not being translated in the same way into action. SEL is in the same boat. There are many educators out there who believe that social-emotional competencies are essential, but because the current incentive structures are continuously focused on academic performance measured by standardized tests, people remain reluctant to get on board the SEL bandwagon. They have trouble seeing how SEL and current assessment demands can coexist.

SEL Is at the Core of All Educational Issues

We have to take a step back and look at the bigger picture and understand that social-emotional development is at the core of any interpersonal issues that a school deals with, regardless of the specifics and details. The school has to use the structure and language that they already have in place so that, whenever something happens in the world, they don't have to have a special assembly. Instead, built-in time and mechanisms are available to talk about these things in a trusted context. That is the most powerful thing of all.

In the past decade, social-emotional learning has focused more attention on urban minority populations. These are populations for which SEL curricula had very rarely been developed in previous research because it was extremely challenging to have randomized control trials in those environments. But they represent environments where there's as much need for SEL and character development as in more advantaged settings.

We found out that if we do not help kids see that they have a sense of positive purpose, there's very little good reason for them to want to learn social competencies or academics. Having a positive goal or purpose and achieving academic success is a package deal. We have come to appreciate deeply and dramatically the fact that we must focus on kids' sense of purpose for them to see hope in the future. It's difficult for kids living in the context of poverty, especially those who worry about their own deportation or the deportation of their family members. It's not easy for them to see a sense of purpose. A lot of kids are walking around with a tremendous sense of pessimism for the future, and it's not necessarily unjustified. Like it or not, this has to be dealt with in the classroom.

Creating a Sense of Agency and Positive Purpose

If we want to inspire kids in urban environments, we must create opportunities in the school for them to have social-emotional competencies and agency and help them begin gradually from there to feel they also have the same agency outside the school as well. To this end, we created our SEL program's student ambassadors. These are students who are elected as peer leaders and actually co-lead SEL lessons. They do positive purpose projects in school and, in many other ways, have a voice when school issues come up. For example, in a school in New Jersey, they had four incidents of kids making mock threats about shooting a teacher or bringing a gun to the school. It wasn't substantiated, and when the kids were eventually interviewed, it turned out they were only kidding. The school's solution was to mobilize their student ambassadors to address the problem because it was an issue of peer culture, peer conversation, and the climate of the school. For adults to come down on this in a heavy-handed way and demand discipline or punishment was not the answer. It wouldn't have solved the underlying issues. Kids need to begin to feel and see their worth, value, and purpose in the school before they're going to be able to carry that out into the future. Simply put, if you want the kids to respect and use SEL, you can't just teach this stuff—you have to live it.

State

How social-emotional learning is advancing is a function of the state you're in. In each state, there is a different threshold and awareness of SEL. In states like Massachusetts and New Jersey, there is a very high public awareness of SEL—many schools have it, and more are examining and implementing it. These states are actually heading toward a tipping point, a critical mass where it's becoming widely accepted and implemented as a standard practice. In other states, SEL isn't present at all. But states like California, Arizona, Connecticut, New York, Ohio, Pennsylvania, Illinois, Washington, Oregon, and others are all developing their internal organizational capacity to support schools in SEL implementation. The idea is to have SEL implemented by state education agencies in the state capitals themselves and then let it spread across additional states from there. That's what it takes—an organized, systematic effort to help implementation—if we're ever going to see this move forward in the way that we all would like. It takes an educational network to make it work. I have not seen an individual school implement and sustain social-emotional learning successfully by itself. That's why I am working with colleagues Jim Vetter and Nova Biro in Massachusetts to establish a national network of state-level SEL advocacy and implementation support organizations called SEL4US.[6]

III. Cost of Maintaining the Status Quo

Here's what we have to recognize: we live in an increasingly complex world that places tremendous demands on individuals as citizens, workers, parents, and community members. We need our teachers to be engaged in more preparation before we feel confident in saying they're ready to implement social-emotional learning with our children. We have folks who are already teaching who need support in building these core SEL competencies. At Rutgers and the College of Saint Elizabeth in Morristown, New Jersey, we have the Academy for Social-Emotional Learning in Schools, which is focused on the expertise of existing teachers and building up their capacity to implement SEL.[7] Additionally, we have the newbies, and there's no way we can prepare them for this unbelievably complex and important job in the extremely limited timeframe that we provide for them during their advanced higher education. This might require a longer post-graduate training period or a longer amount of time in school itself.

It's also equally important that change happens with educational administrators because they determine what occurs in a school. A teacher could already be doing SEL in the classroom, but if the administrator doesn't know about it or is not interested and supportive, then all the wonderful work does not lead to anything systematic. It's not only a matter of the teachers and students; effective SEL encompasses the entire education system, including custodians, office personnel, and cafeteria staff. Everyone in the building needs to reinforce the practice. The Academy therefore addresses school leaders along with teachers.

If SEL isn't taught in the home, then the school cannot be entirely effective in teaching it. The only way the school can be beneficial is if a unified voice exists among the teachers, the students, the parents, and the school staff. Then it will get its message across in an efficient and all-encompassing way. The secret is that teaching the unified voice must take place over multiple years, just as it does in reading, math, science, and social studies. If you widely vary your curriculum and your pedagogy from year to year, you're not going to get much uptake on the part of kids. The same holds true for SEL.

We have it within our power to avoid becoming fragmented by seeing every individual issue as isolated and separate. We can begin to look at how all these social problems and concerns are examples of SEL and character development that need attention. Students on the fringes think, "Why should I be involved in SEL if I don't have any positive aspirations for the future? Why should I be involved in thinking about long-term consequences if I don't anticipate any good long-term consequences in my life? And why should I trust these teachers who are trying to teach this stuff if I've been hurt by adults in the past?" Helping kids attain a state of forgiveness, compassion, and gratitude is part and parcel of opening them up to learning social-emotional competencies and seeing that they have the potential for a bright future.

IV. Forecast for the Future

When we've seen successful implementation and sustainability, it happened because those schools were connected to other schools doing SEL. The widespread implementation support system turns out to be a necessary ingredient for SEL to be carried out systematically. An individual school may be able to do it for a little bit by itself, but people leave, leadership changes, the board changes, an issue of the day enters in and takes over, and SEL becomes difficult to sustain. I have not seen a school implement and sustain SEL by itself, but when SEL implementation is part of a larger movement or practice, it's a different story.

An important element necessary for a school to implement SEL successfully is an improved culture and climate. The school should be a building where both adults and children feel welcomed and enjoy. It should be a place that brings a sense of purpose, pride, and contribution. Those are common characteristics in schools that support the social-emotional, character, and academic growth of children, and that's a metric you can apply when visiting or assessing schools. If a school says they're implementing SEL but fails to have a positive climate, they're not doing it the right way. The climate and culture have got to be essential elements of the SEL implementation.

The other thing you'll see in a successful implementation is a common language. You'll see that the language of SEL is not isolated to the SEL class. For instance, if SEL is taught for a 45-minute period once a week or three times a week for 20 minutes, the language has a way of stretching outside the confines of the class. You will see artifacts on classroom walls. You will see posters and sayings in the halls and cafeteria. You will hear people using the prompts and cues of SEL to bring the skills out in the kids. You will hear it happening in classes where it's not being taught. You will go into a social studies class or a language arts class, and you'll hear people talking about feelings and relationships using the SEL lexicon. These are the indicators of a building that has taken on social-emotional learning.

When you implement an SEL curriculum, you've got to bring it in with intentionality. You've got to bring it in with the understanding that you're building a set of important life skills. But what does it mean to develop a skill? You don't build a skill in a very general way; you have to build a skill in a specific, structured way. Almost every SEL curriculum that is worth anything has a self-regulatory component. It teaches some type of emotional regulation skill. For example, the Social Decision Making/Problem Solving program uses the phrase "Keep Calm."[8] It isn't a generic statement; it is a practice. In the curriculum, "Keep Calm" is taught as a series of steps that kids deliberately undertake. If I want a student to invoke a self-calming procedure, I can't tell the student, "Calm yourself down." I can't tell the student, "Be calm." I can't tell the student, "Take a deep breath." I have to tell the student, "Use 'Keep Calm,'" and they will then move through the procedures of the "Keep Calm" skill set they've been taught. I have to make an effort to correctly identify and prompt the skill set that I want the kids to use.

That is a discipline that only comes when people have a shared under-standing of the mission and a common language. That's the main reason why we don't see the "stickiness" in some of the SEL curricula being implemented. They haven't taken steps to make sure the principles of that curriculum are followed outside of the SEL instructional environment. Failing to make SEL and its language a standard part of the school day is the single biggest issue and obstacle to long-term successful and effective implementation.

Obviously, we want to extend SEL outside of the school and into the homes too. When the families and the school are aligned in building SEL competen-cies, it's a great thing. We wrote *Emotionally Intelligent Parenting* based on that premise.[9] Let's give the families the tools and skills at home to reinforce the SEL instruction in the school. But what if they don't? Then they don't. It mirrors the old days of parenting, when the ability of parents to help kids with academics was very limited. Many parents couldn't read English while their kids were learning to read in school.

An average school year is 180 days, so a school has that many opportunities every year to influence children. If they implement SEL successfully, the kids are going to learn the SEL skills with or without family involvement. The kids are also going to learn to code-switch with SEL just like they do with everything else. They might not be using their SEL skills at home as much as they're using them in the school, but if they use them in school and learn to use them in in college and the workplace, they're going to be in pretty good shape. That's our goal.

V. Pathway to Success

I think we have reached SEL 2.0, a version of SEL which necessarily includes character development. We now recognize the need to be explicit about what previously has been implicit in SEL by acknowledging that SEL is not value-neutral. Nobody wants to have socially and emotionally skilled, smart children with poor character. I refer to current social-emotional and character development as SEL 2.0 because it necessarily brings in the character piece of the puzzle.

We have to be ready and willing to stand by the fact that there are certain values and virtues that schools intentionally need to promote. When you talk to teachers, by and large, they've gone into education because they want to help kids become better people. Being "better people" includes being responsible, having integrity, being cooperative and caring, and being supportive of others. When these basic values are implicit in SEL curricula, then, by its very nature, SEL suppresses bullying. When we talk about SEL 2.0, we're not talking about something that's value-neutral; we're talking about a philosophy and curricula that have an implicit value structure linked to caring, kindness, consideration, cooperation, and mutual support. It creates a school culture and climate that exemplifies those attributes.

That's why I talk about SEL 2.0. That's why we can't disconnect social-emotional competencies from character virtues and a positive purpose. In a religious school context—and there are religious schools of various faiths that focus on SEL to some degree—there is a positive purpose philosophy naturally built in. There are wonderful examples of schools that show the social-emotional competencies being used and not used by various religious characters within their scripture. In the public education environment, a sense of positive purpose is something that we must work toward actively inspiring in our kids. Many of our kids have gone down a dark path, driven to a sense of negative purpose by their home and outside environment. It's understandable, but we have to combat it in the classroom and in the school.

One of the other things sometimes glossed over is that, according to a meta-analysis done by Joseph Durlak in collaboration with CASEL, the strongest successes have been associated with at least two years of implementation.[10] Often, when we talk about SEL, we do it without specifying dosage and saturation, or even defining what those things are. Many of us would agree that, for something to be called social-emotional learning, it has to be implemented for a minimum of thirty to forty-five minutes a week for an entire school year. Experience has shown that this is the absolute minimum required to affect the culture. If it doesn't have that minimum dosage, it's very difficult to say that a school even has an SEL structure in place.

And even that minimum dosage becomes insufficient if it doesn't include the prompts and informal reinforcers used by cafeteria workers, custodians, and office staff. These people are necessary to embed social-emotional learning into the everyday school routine. If we only have SEL in SEL class, then we can't say we truly have social-emotional competence schoolwide. It has to become a pervasive part of what happens in a school, and it should be obvious to an observer. We should be able to look for it and find it in the hallways. Sometimes implementation is successful, and sometimes it's not, but either way it shouldn't be considered an indictment of the SEL program itself—it is a statement about the implementation. No program is implementation proof, but we have enough evidence supporting SEL programs to prove their effectiveness if they are implemented consistently throughout the school.

An analogy about reading is a perfect example. If we only read during reading class, we wouldn't say that we have true literacy. We've always known that literacy is essential, but we are heading to a point as a society where we recognize its gravity. Reading is so critically important as a necessary skill that, in fact, if you cannot read, you're going to be extremely hampered in what you can accomplish in life. In the same way, if you can't read people, if you can't interpret situations, if you can't read feelings and emotional cues, you are going to be hindered in what you can accomplish in your life even if you have an incredibly high IQ. These are abilities that can be—and should be—taught, and it's going to be recognized more and more on a broader scale that these social-emotional competencies are as basic to human functionality in society as foundational mathematical and linguistic skills.

When SEL is done in a systematic way, there is a very high likelihood of seeing good results at the end. We don't always get results in one year, and we may not even get them in two. Typically, though, we see real results and a major culture change by year three. The secret is to make sure that we have the proper support and benchmarks for good implementation.

Editor's Reflection Questions

- In your experience, can SEL be effective if it's not present in both the school and the home? What about other organizations within the community? If not, how do we ensure it is a part of each setting?
- Has your school set aside dedicated time to focus solely on SEL? If not, what benefits do you think you're missing? If yes, how have you taken advantage of this time?
- Where have you seen gaps in SEL buy-in and implementation at the district, state, or national level? What must we do as an education community to push SEL buy-in past the tipping point?

NOTES

1. Maurice Elias, Michael Gara, Peggy A. Rothbaum, Ann M. Reese, and Michael Ubriaco. "A multivariate analysis of factors differentiating behaviorally and emotionally dysfunctional children from other groups in school." *Journal of Clinical Child Psychology* 16, no. 4 (1987): 107-112.

2. Daniel Goleman. *Emotional Intelligence: Why It Can Matter More Than IQ.* (New York: Bantam, 1995).

3. For more information about CASEL, see *casel.org.*

4. Joseph E. Zins, Maurice Elias, Roger P. Weissberg, Karin S. Frey, Mark T. Greenberg, Norris M. Haynes, Rachael Kessler, Mary E. Schwab-Stone, and Timothy P. Shriver. *Promoting Social and Emotional Learning: Guidelines for Educators.* (Alexandria: ASCD, 1997).

5. For more information about ASCD, see *www.ascd.org.*

6. For more information about SEL4US, see *www.sel4ma.org/sel4us/.*

7. For more information about the Academy for Social-Emotional Learning in Schools, see *SELinschools.org.*

8. For more information about the Social Decision Making/Problem Solving Program for SEL, see *ubhc.rutgers.edu/sdm/.*

9. Maurice J. Elias, Steven E. Tobias, and Brian S. Friedlander. *Emotionally Intelligent Parenting: How to Raise a Self-Disciplined, Responsible, Socially Skilled Child.* (New York: Harmony, 1999).

10. Joseph A. Durlak, Roger P. Weissberg, Allison B. Dymnicki, Rhys D. Taylor, and Kriston B. Schellinger. "The impact of enhancing students' social and emotional learning: A meta-analysis of school-based universal interventions." *Child Development* 82, no. 1 (2011): 405–432.

Dorothy Espelage

ESTABLISHING SEL PRACTICES TO DRIVE LONG-TERM SUCCESS

Dorothy Espelage, PhD, is Professor of Psychology at the University of Florida. She is the recipient of the American Psychological Association's Lifetime Achievement Award in Prevention Science and its 2016 Award for Distinguished Contributions to Research in Public Policy. Over the last 20 years, she has authored over 140 peer reviewed articles, five books, and thirty chapters on bullying, homophobic teasing, sexual harassment, dating violence, and gang violence.

I. CURRENT STATE OF SEL

Social-emotional learning (SEL) was introduced at a conference hosted by the Fetzer Institute in 1994.[1] A group of researchers, practitioners, and policymakers came together at this conference, and they collectively created this umbrella term. The definition of SEL included a lot of things that were already out there in the field at the time—social skills, coping skills, and character education were all already popular topics—but this term gave everyone an easier way to talk about how all these skill sets can be developed alongside one another. Since that time, there has been some significant progress in developing social-emotional learning programs and curricula informed by all of the evidence and data gathered by researchers, but in my opinion, the most significant developments have been made in determining how to evaluate the efficacy of these social-emotional learning programs once they are introduced and implemented in schools.

Local

What we found with several meta-analyses in the last few years is that, once kids are exposed to developmentally appropriate social-emotional learning consistently in K–12 settings, they have less destructive behavior in the classroom and higher academic scores. We're at a point now where programs are grounded in the evidence and research.

What we're trying to understand is how to tailor these programs to fit the local context, the cultural setting, and the changing demographics in our classrooms all across the country. There are many core common components to SEL, but we also know that there has to be some tailoring at the local level. Social-emotional learning will look different in Classroom A than it does in Classroom B and different in School A than it does in School B. Social-emotional learning may look different in the South Side of Chicago than it does in a high-resource, affluent suburb just outside of Chicago. We have evidence-based, research-informed programs that can range from classroom curriculum to after-school programs to make social-emotional learning become embedded within the arts in our school. How do we tailor them to address the challenges that we have in the school system, whether it's equity or discipline issues?

We also need to understand how to prepare teachers to develop their own social-emotional learning competencies so they can teach it in the classroom. We have to recognize that many of our new teachers are coming in ill-equipped with their own social-emotional learning competencies and need to be brought up to speed quickly. There's been a lot of attention on how we take the programs that we're giving kids and adolescents and adapt them so our pre-service and future teachers in higher education institutions across the United States can develop competencies before getting into the classroom.

We have also discovered that the depth of SEL needs to grow beyond the classroom. Some of the first people in a school who need to be well versed in social-emotional learning are the school office staff, cafeteria staff, and the school resource officer assigned by local law enforcement. Disciplinary cases going through the administrative personnel commonly originate in the cafeteria, where the uniformed school resource officers are on the front lines as walking SEL ambassadors and reinforcers.

Regional

Defining social-emotional learning by its five different domains—self-awareness, self-management, social awareness, relationship skills, and responsible decision-making—we've tracked the impact SEL has had on students past their public school career. We know that kids who were exposed to the SEL environment in early childhood and elementary school years see very favorable outcomes decades later, whether it's higher career aspirations or fewer mental health challenges. Business and industry leaders need to see SEL not as just soft skills, but also as fundamental skills that help create a very successful workforce through practiced teamwork, enhanced creativity, and successful conflict resolution.

There have been regional and state movements where the policymakers have placed social-emotional learning as a priority for funding of research and programming to address school safety issues. We need progressive legislation that provides adequate funding and resources for school districts to partner with scholars to develop the best ways to address K–12 social-emotional learning programs, but we also need to keep an eye on implementation science and sustainability. It comes down to budgets; it's all about the money, the support, and the creating time in a day given to teachers, students, and administrators to build that foundational SEL skill set.

Social-emotional learning, for the most part, isn't seen yet as a universal thing that everybody needs within the context of our schools and classrooms. The mental health field talks more about directed types of intervention that are more specific, but we think the community can benefit long-term from social-emotional learning in the mental health realm by thinking of universal prevention. School psychologists and social workers still have the approach where a crisis must exist for a child before services go into effect. There needs to be a shift toward prevention, as opposed to reactive intervention.

Mental health practitioners have to be put back into schools. A lot of mental health programming in our schools has been taken away because of budget constraints and society's prejudice against mental health conditions and issues. Administrators also need to be able to give the mental health professionals the space to do their work, and they should not just be reacting to things when they go wrong. Instead, they need to be proactive to prevent things from happening. Mental health professionals and advocates at the national level keep talking about a reduction of risks, but they forget that when you reduce risks, it doesn't create protection. The absence of risk doesn't mean there's protection, and protective factors need to be created in the space deliberately and consciously.

State

As advocates of social-emotional learning, we are acutely aware that our messaging in regard to SEL doesn't resonate with all of America. As much as we in the education community embrace SEL, disparate groups are attacking it all across the country. Recently, while advising a state agency on updating their health education standards, SEL experts were informed that social-emotional learning is not a phrase that they could use to define or describe this education standard in their state. The staffers involved said that elected members of the state and federal legislatures believed that social-emotional learning is "brainwashing of our children."

In front of lawmakers like these, we need to talk about workforce development and the very skills that are going to make our kids successful in vocational trade schools, college or university, or the workplace. We talk about academic outcomes as well as the soft skills that we're championing in social-emotional learning. But the bottom line is that, to the politicians and the parents that elected them, test scores and accountability—from the classroom teacher level all the way up to the school district level—are always going to be very important.

SEL researchers need to collect academic outcome data because that's what speaks to politicians. The Durlak meta-analysis in 2011 got attention from both sides of the aisle in Washington, D.C., because of a couple of striking findings.[2] First, researchers were able to document that there's less disruption in the classroom with SEL programs in place. The research clearly showed that teachers involved in SEL programs remained in the profession who otherwise would have quit teaching entirely because of the disruptions in the classroom due to conduct and discipline issues they would have faced on a daily basis without SEL practices. But what really got the attention and the support from both sides of the aisle was the data that showed a kid who is exposed to social-emotional learning programming had test scores that are 11% higher on average than a kid who was not exposed to SEL in the classroom.

There are many advantages, but the main selling points to budget officers and committee members on the state level really should be about keeping kids engaged in the classroom, creating safer classrooms so fewer teachers drop out of the profession, and ensuring higher graduation rates from high school. All of these ultimately lead to a stronger and better workforce.

II. Cost of Maintaining the Status Quo

Research shows that children from early elementary school ages up through adolescence are experiencing the highest rates of daily anxiety and angst that researchers have seen in a long time.[3-5] We need to better communicate to parents the social-emotional programming that's happening in schools to help reduce the trauma students are bringing into the classroom from outside the building.

We hear over and over from parents that they have no idea that many administrators have a particular social-emotional learning program going on in a classroom. The percentage of parents who have no idea of what's going on at school is shocking, and as a field of scholars and educational practitioners, we need to do a better job of communicating what's happening in the school to the home, so parents have the opportunity to reinforce the messaging around SEL. Translating the exercises and the role plays performed in the classroom into real-world scenarios called "teachable moments" is critically important. Students are attempting to pull out those practices, skills, and information to use them as a bridge to solve problems in their lives.

Involved parents in the K–12 setting also see the benefits early on and talk with their kids about how to regulate their emotions, communicate, and prevent conflict. We need to do a better job of creating a parent-intervention program so that they also have those skills and can use them to reinforce their children's learning. We have to communicate better so that we can work together in tandem with parents to give them the opportunity to contribute to the reinforcement of things happening in our school, or else nothing will change.

A study has shown that 28% of the kids in schools are "not engaged," and 17% are "actively disengaged."[6] These are disengaged kids who do not have one trusted adult in the building. Some have trusted adults at home but no one to connect to in school. These kids come from all walks of life, all ethnic groups, economic levels, cultures, and genders. They're not in clubs, not in sporting games; maybe they have to go home and take care of their siblings, work in the family business, or help support the family after school. We have found places where the undocumented students just disengage because they fear any attention.

Some of our kids experience this extreme social isolation with the heightened anxiety that studies show is so prevalent these days.[7-8] As much as we talk about random acts of kindness, we as a society are very comfortable with isolated people, and we are not reaching out to them. The social isolation that is so common in our schools is compounded by the fact that there are many adults in school systems who feel okay with isolated kids as long as those kids are not making any trouble. To avoid any risk of a confrontation, they are just not inquiring and seeing how that kid is doing, and as a result, a significant proportion of the student population is isolated.

Some teachers will say, "Well, the school is so big," but that's not an excuse. It's our fault for creating schools that are big, but you can have a cohesive school that's big. You just build smaller communities within it. We have fundamental and instinctual need for trusting and loving human relationships. That's not the case for a number of the kids in our school buildings, even with an SEL program in place.

III. Forecast for the Future

We're at a point now where after decades of research and practice we have programs that are rooted in evidence and founded on solid research. The challenge is to think about implementation and sustainability over time while remaining sensitive to the developmental nuances of SEL as kids age in the K–12 setting and beyond.

We recognize that kids exposed to social-emotional learning see their test scores improve dramatically, but we also need to acknowledge that there are long-term, and not just short-term, benefits. The ultimate long-term outcomes for these adults show a lower incidence of mental health issues, better employment, less unemployment, and fewer domestic violence incidents. We see these results early on and decades later, and they lead to improvements in our workforce and a lower number of people utilizing mental health facilities and scarce community resources.

One of the challenges is finding space and time for the SEL work. For instance, Second Step is an SEL program in middle school.[9] It includes 15 lessons that cover the five domains of social-emotional learning, and they exist in that format and in that order for a reason. The program and lessons are designed to be delivered and taught in a particular way and in a specific sequence to be effective. A social worker is only given three hours a week or three hours in a semester to cover SEL, so they're picking a few scattered lessons from the program to teach and implement—that's all they have time to do. As a result, the lessons are out of order and isolated from each other. Rather than building upon progress, the lessons skip essential skills and coping mechanisms. The 15 lessons are implemented in a piecemeal fashion that goes against the developmental sequencing that was carefully built into the program and defeats the effectiveness of the SEL program. And this happens just because we didn't make time to teach it.

We also need to engage with how we leverage all this great technology that we have in order to reinforce some of those tenets or components of social-emotional learning. We need to think about leveraging technology because that's where the kids live. We've developed a text-messaging program for middle school students that reinforces the ideas developed in role-playing in the classroom curriculum. They are able to understand these skills in real time as they have a conflict with a sibling because a text message comes in asking, "What are some different ways that you can cope with this?" It's very interactive; they can win certificates and badges. As a result of the availability of inexpensive technology, a lot of beneficial vintage social-emotional learning programs that were just sitting in three-ring binders can be redeveloped to be available in a much more technology-savvy way on electronic platforms.

As we look at social-emotional learning of the future, we've begun to combine it with trauma-informed approaches. We are giving professional development to our teachers and staff that includes trauma-based instruction. Teachers and administrators are taught to manage problematic behavior by seeing it through a new trauma-informed lens.

Also, in the very near future, we're going to start hearing about equity and diversity as an SEL outcome. How do we address equity issues in education, and can we do that within the social-emotional learning framework? We're going to start hearing conversations about the need to push the framework of social-emotional learning to address diversity and inequity in the classroom and the community. In the future, it's all about SEL having a broader and longer impact that brings about more justice within education.

IV. Pathway to Success

We need to focus a lot of energy on developing social-emotional programming and frameworks for kids in the future, as classroom and community dynamics evolve and change. Educators need effective and timely professional development to stay abreast of the latest trends, research, and procedures. Communications pathways need to connect successfully and effectively with the parents and families at home.

As the Durlak study has shown, when we talk to folks in the field as they are implementing programs or approaches as intended, there is not only an improvement in students' academic achievement, but there's also an improvement in the perceptions of a general environment of safety within the school.[10] Research shows that successful implementation reduces homophobic name-calling, bullying, and sexual harassment with social-emotional learning programs.[11-14] Separate research shows these are all precursors to intimate partner violence and other types of violence that we see later on in life.[15]

Educators at all different levels need to be familiarized with social-emotional learning. They need to understand their own social-emotional learning competencies. Some naturally do it, and they have been doing it their entire careers, even before the term "social-emotional learning" was coined. There also needs to be ongoing training, openness, and recognition of what SEL is system-wide. Do the secretaries in the office use the language when the kids are sitting there waiting to be disciplined? Are there opportunities where everybody in the room is using SEL language? Is that happening in the cafeteria as well? It's one thing for it to happen in the classroom, but we need the spillover to other areas that we call the "reach" of the program and philosophy. It's not just teachers. Often, principals and assistant principals have had very little to almost zero training in child development, and they don't necessarily understand social-emotional learning at the same level as their teachers or students. They need professional development as well to develop their SEL skill sets. All of the adults in the building need to recognize that there has to be continual practice, reinforcement, and redundancy for SEL to stick in the child's mind.

With SEL in place, teachers and students feel more connected in the school. There are deeper relationships between the students and the teachers. There are more trusted adults that the students can communicate with openly, so the students feel valued and heard. Thus, because the kids feel safer, there is better academic performance. The teachers, in turn, feel more competent within the classroom, there's more ownership of the climate in school by the students and teachers, and research shows that trickles into the families at home as well.

SEL has to go beyond the individual child to make sure that all adults who interact with the children also have the same social-emotional competencies; otherwise, they're not going to be able to teach and reinforce it. Increasingly, we're challenged to do parenting intervention. We're starting to see more social-emotional learning programs and interventions that target the family system and dynamics. We talk to kids about empathy, perspective-taking, belly breathing, and mindfulness. They take these lessons home to families where many of these parents have never had exposure to social-emotional learning. In the best-case scenarios, we've seen kids who have developed really good ways to regulate their emotions share these skills and lessons with their parents, who then use them when they get upset. For SEL to make the ultimate difference, we need to get parental outreach programs into the home so that we can all have access to the common language that reinforces learning.

Editor's Reflection Questions

- Who are the SEL ambassadors and reinforcers in your school or organization? How can they be effective at maintaining fidelity and commitment to social-emotional support for all?

- Consider the five domains of SEL—self-awareness, self-management, social awareness, relationship skills, and responsible decision-making. Think about their importance to students' short-term success and how they contribute to long-term success as kids become adults. Are you intentionally addressing each of these in your learners?

- If there was no evidence SEL improved academic performance, would your perspective on it change? How does the research showing the impact of SEL on academics add to your urgency for integration?

NOTES

1. "History," CASEL, accessed March 27, 2018, *https://casel.org/history/.*

2. Joseph A. Durlak, Roger P. Weissberg, Allison B. Dymnicki, Rhys D. Taylor, and Kriston B. Schellinger. "The impact of enhancing students' social and emotional learning: A meta-analysis of school-based universal interventions." *Child Development* 82, no. 1 (2011): 405–432.

3. Jean M. Twenge. "Time period and birth cohort differences in depressive symptoms in the US, 1982–2013." *Social Indicators Research* 121, no. 2 (2015): 437-454.

4. Jean M. Twenge, Brittany Gentile, C. Nathan DeWall, Debbie Ma, Katharine Lacefield, and David R. Schurtz. "Birth cohort increases in psychopathology among young Americans, 1938–2007: A cross-temporal meta-analysis of the MMPI." *Clinical Psychology Review* 30, no. 2 (2010): 145–154.

5. Jean M. Twenge. "The age of anxiety? The birth cohort change in anxiety and neuroticism, 1952–1993." *Journal of Personality and Social Psychology* 79, no. 6 (2000): 1007–1021.

6. Gary Gordon, "School leadership linked to engagement and student achievement," Gallup, accessed March 26, 2018, *http://www.gallup.com/services/176711/school-leadership-linked-engagement-student-achievement.aspx.*

7. "Any Anxiety Disorder," National Institute of Mental Health, accessed March 26, 2018, *https://www.nimh.nih.gov/health/statistics/any-anxiety-disorder.shtml#part_155096.*

8. Kathleen Ries Merikangas, Jian-ping He, Marcy Burstein, Sonja A. Swanson, Shelli Avenevoli, Lihong Cui, Corina Benjet, Katholiki Georgiades, and Joel Swendsen. "Lifetime prevalence of mental disorders in U.S. adolescents: results from the National Comorbidity Survey Replication--Adolescent Supplement (NCS-A)." *Journal of the American Academy of Child and Adolescent Psychiatry* 49, no. 10 (2010): 980–989.

9. Learn more about the Second Step program at *http://www.secondstep.org/second-step-social-emotional-learning.*

10. Durlak et al. "The impact of enhancing students' social and emotional learning: A meta-analysis of school-based universal interventions."

11. Dorothy L. Espelage, Mark Van Ryzin, Sabina Low, and Joshua Polanin. "Clinical trial of Second Step© middle-school Program: Impact on bullying, cyberbullying, homophobic teasing and sexual harassment perpetration." *School Psychology Review* 44, no. 4 (2015): 464–479.

12. Dorothy L. Espelage, Chad A. Rose, and Joshua R. Polanin. "Social-emotional learning program to promote prosocial and academic skills among middle school students with disabilities." *Remedial and Special Education* 37, no. 6 (2016): 323–332.

13. Dorothy L. Espelage, Chad A. Rose., and Joshua R. Polanin. "Social-emotional learning program to reduce bullying, fighting, and victimization among middle school students with disabilities." *Remedial and Special Education* 36, no. 5 (2015): 299–311.

14. Dorothy L. Espelage, Sabina Low, Joshua R. Polanin, M.A., and Eric C. Brown. "Clinical trial of Second Step© middle-school program: Impact on aggression & victimization." *Journal of Applied Developmental Psychology* 37 (2015): 52–63.

15. Nadine M. Connell, Robert G. Morris, and Alex R. Piquero. "Predicting Bullying: Exploring the Contributions of Childhood Negative Life Experiences in Predicting Adolescent Bullying Behavior." *International Journal of Offender Therapy and Comparative Criminology* 60, no. 9 (2016) 1082-1096.

Sean Slade

PROVIDING WELL-ROUNDED SUPPORT TO FULFILL THE PROMISE OF EDUCATION

Sean Slade is the Senior Director of Global Outreach at ASCD. He has written extensively on topics related to whole child education, and he has been at the forefront of promoting and using school climate, connectedness, resilience, and a youth development focus for school improvement. He has been a teacher, department head, educational researcher, senior education officer, and director in Australia, Italy, Venezuela, the United Kingdom, and the United States.

I. CURRENT STATE OF SEL

We are at an excellent point in time regarding well-rounded education, and educational philosophy is changing the way social-emotional learning (SEL) is implemented in the school setting.

We structure and frame social-emotional learning within our Whole Child approach at ASCD (formerly known as the Association for Supervision and Curriculum Development).[1] It acts as an umbrella under which SEL lives; it's the focus of the "what" and "why" of where we want kids to be when they graduate. We want to educate them as whole people and whole individuals. You're not just teaching them academically and cognitively, but also socially, emotionally, mentally, and physically. Our approach strives to enhance learning by addressing each student's needs through the shared contributions of schools, families, communities, and policymakers. It's an understanding that we are trying to develop, nurture, and educate the complete child more than just the academic portion.

ASCD sees social-emotional learning as part of that larger framework. The definition of what is required of students as future leaders of society is less about academic content knowledge and more about understanding social skills, dynamic group skills, leadership skills, and creative problem-solving skills that bring with them the ability to cope with adversity and obstacles. The core skills and attributes that kids are going to need in this century and beyond are the abilities to bring people into a collaboration, to be part of a group, and to gain the knowledge and confidence to lead that group if need be.

I used to be a social studies and science teacher, but my main content area was physical education. When I taught physical education, I was always very concerned about the development of what at that time were referred to as "character skills." I emphasized teamwork, leadership, and raising the self-esteem and self-efficacy of kids. I was far less concerned about the actual skills or activities than I was about the person behind it all. It was amazing to be able to change someone who is lacking in self-confidence or understanding of their own capacity by using one or two simple activities. To get them engaged and watch them all of a sudden do something that they thought was impossible half an hour before, whether it was swimming, gymnastics, or accomplishing some complex activity—this became life-changing for both me and the students.

I was teaching back in the 1990s at an international school in northern Italy. I had a mixed class of grades 4 and 5, and when I taught them, it inevitably wound up in arguments and general misbehavior. It was not only annoying, but also extremely frustrating. I stopped teaching the standard course and ended up devising a brand-new unit based on teamwork, leadership, and problem-solving—in short, similar to a team-based video game. I devised eight stages focused on activities like trying to transport somebody from one part of the gymnasium to the other or trying to get somebody over a ledge, and each one was to develop a different part of the person and a different skill for the team. I put all of the kids in small groups and then mixed them up so that each group had different heights, sizes, genders, strengths, and weaknesses. I made sure to switch activities at each stage to ensure that every person who was part of the team was essential at some point. In each lesson, the teams had a level or two with specific goals to get through, and if they weren't able to complete the activity, they were required to go back, rethink, replan, and try again. In each of the stages, they had to develop and work on their team skills, cooperation skills, problem-solving skills, and creativity skills to solve a problem.

We did it for about a month, and at the end, I asked the kids to give me feedback on the program. The feedback I received was so perfect you would have sworn I'd given the answers to the kids. They said things like "I learned that if we don't succeed, we have to go back, rethink, and try again" and "I learned that we all have our skills and we all have our time when we can succeed" and "I learned that even though I might be the loudest, I need to listen to other people in order to get the best answer" and "I learned that we need to keep trying things in different variations to overcome obstacles and succeed." It was wonderful!

After we went back to the more standard physical education curriculum, we found that students took it upon themselves to address many of the behaviors and conflict issues they had learned to address in groups during that single month. As a result, the conflicts and behavioral problems that had at one time been rampant in the classroom dramatically decreased. By improving their collaboration skills, problem-solving skills, and self-efficacy, that unit affected everything else that they did from that point on in the year.

That was a clarifying and crystallizing moment for me. I realized that the social-emotional skill set is essential and that it must be incorporated as a practice integrated into all the lessons and activities taught from then on, not just as a stand-alone unit. ASCD's Whole Child approach focuses attention on the social, emotional, mental, physical, and cognitive development of each child. We believe that social-emotional learning needs to spread throughout every facet of the school. All subjects and content areas need to incorporate and infuse social-emotional learning.

Teachers don't want an additional thing added on to their workload without something else being taken away because they're continually being asked to do more and more. What we can show educators is that social-emotional learning actually helps teaching and aids in the learning process in the classroom. It reduces some of the behavior issues, and it increases not only student-to-school connectedness, but also teacher-to-school connectedness.

From a whole child education perspective, we are at the very start of a new era in which schools, districts, parents, and policymakers are starting to look at education as being more than just academics. Education practice and policy tends to swing like a pendulum: one decade this way, the next decade that way. With No Child Left Behind, we've been in a decade of academics for the sake of academics.[2] This next decade will hopefully be the dawning of understanding that schools need to have a more holistic approach to learning and that they have a huge role in the development of well-rounded citizens. We need to develop the macro skills like collaboration, creativity, and problem-solving that a good citizen needs to possess to become a productive and valued member of their community. As educators, parents, and communities, we need to prepare our students to be useful members of society and ready for the future that lies ahead.

State

The Collaborative for Academic, Social, and Emotional Learning (CASEL) is a highly respected organization in state and federal legislatures and has done a great job in mobilizing their forces and engaging school districts and politicians.[3] Because of their efforts, you're seeing states like Massachusetts and Kentucky focusing on social-emotional learning as a core part of their state education policy.

As educators, we need to get our policymakers and the heads of our departments of education at both the state and federal level to have a frank and honest discussion about what makes a successful student. A successful student is not always necessarily the one proficient in language arts and mathematics or who possesses a high GPA.

And we are seeing a range of organizations become more involved in the whole child nationally. For example, the Chan Zuckerberg Initiative has recently launched its "whole-child personalized learning" focus.[4] The Robert Wood Johnson Foundation is a strong backer of aligning health and education and has helped support the Whole School, Whole Community, Whole Child (WSCC) model.[5] The Every Student Succeeds Act (ESSA), signed into law in 2015, has a requirement for nonacademic statewide evaluation, and currently 12 states have written our Whole Child approach or WSCC model into their ESSA state plans.[6]

Global

The same discussions are occurring overseas as well. The Organiztion for Economic Co-operation and Development (OECD), which administers the Programme for International Student Assessment (PISA) every three years, is leading a global working group called the Future of Education and Skills 2030.[7-8] This group, which ASCD is a part of, is developing what education policies should and will look like as we move toward 2030. The primary objective they are working toward is the ultimate goal of individual and collective well-being.

OECD and the global community have picked up this mantra of education as more than just academics. For example, the OECD has incorporated measurements for the skills of collaboration and cooperation into PISA, and they are integrating global competencies including social-emotional well-being in PISA from next year onward because they see a demand and need for those competencies in the future.

II. Cost of Maintaining the Status Quo

It may seem a bit cliché, but in my talks and keynotes, I ask my audiences of school health professionals, principals, and teachers to describe a child at 25 years old. It could be their child, it could be someone they teach, or it could be someone they taught in the past. I ask them to describe a character-istic of that child in one word. Essentially, it puts the onus back on the stake-holders to define what they want the child to look like when maturing into society at large. They come up with similar responses: happy, healthy, com-passionate, empathetic, resourceful, caring, and so forth. And when you ask parents, they will come up with the same responses.

The difficulty comes in when you have parents who believe in a more antiquated version of traditional schooling in which the family and the parents take care of the social-emotional side and the school takes care of the academic and cognitive side. It's a reasonable discussion, and my response very often is that I'm pleased those skills and traits are being picked up by the family and the local community, but social-emotional well-being should not be handled by either the school or the family alone, but by a combination of both.

The skill set that society and industry are asking for and that the OECD is defining are the skills of creativity, problem-solving, collaboration, and communication. These skills prepare children to be productive in society. If we don't develop those skills, then the child will be at a disadvantage when they leave high school and enter the world. Allowing and encouraging parents and the community to have input into what they expect their child to look like at the end of schooling empowers them. It ends up being a much more fruitful discussion when everyone affected in the community participates.

Too often, the last time parents were in a high school may have been at their high school graduation. They may have an incorrect understanding that high schools are just as they were in the 1970s, 1980s, or 1990s. Some schools may still look like that, but a lot of schools have moved on and changed the way they're teaching. They have changed philosophies, they have upgraded the courses, and they have improved the way they're engaging with the stu-dents. The pushback you get from parents or community is often from a dated understanding of what schooling looks like.

Despite that pushback, SEL practitioners are gaining entry into the school and implementing its practices across the school curriculum. Unfortunately, we have some programs and entities out there that try and showcase social-emotional learning as only an add-on curriculum or program as opposed to a complete transformation of how a school can look. That approach may act as a decent start to the discussion or even begin the teaching and learning, but merely having a social-emotional learning program once a month for eight hours or a once a year program for eight weeks is not enough.

We have to ensure that SEL doesn't devolve into a programmatic entry for teachers. We can't make teachers think, "Here are an additional five things I need to teach, and I'm the only person that has to do it." We must make sure it engages the entire educational structure. We reinforce the idea of overall school change. We want schools to change and help involve parents and the community in teaching the core skills that help students become productive citizens moving into the next century.

There is a continuous discussion in education about what education should be. There are a lot of people involved in the education industry that have a very myopic idea and view of education. It's often because their industry or their organization is based on an outdated concept or obsolete vision. There are a lot of curricula and publications that still support outdated educational concepts. A holistic SEL education should be a permanent entity for the development of the whole child into a good citizen, but SEL is continuously fighting against vested and historical interests.

The pendulum of public opinion and political pressure that swings back and forth over decades between academics and social-emotional learning—and that is currently open to the development of the whole child and SEL—is going to eventually swing back to academics if we don't convince the public that SEL matters. It may not turn as far from SEL as it did the past decade, but we are eventually going to get a swing back to academic and cognitive demands. To mitigate this pendulum swing, we need to make sure that SEL is not only part of the standard state and federal policies, but also part of the culture of education. We must make sure that when the pendulum swings back again, social-emotional learning isn't wiped clean as just another sporadic fad.

One of the biggest barriers to making sure social-emotional learning and whole child education gets embedded into the culture of education is the way we assess schools and students. Our assessment practices are still based on high-stakes standardized test scores in a very small range of subject areas, and that needs to change. The ongoing debate isn't about whether or not you can assess social-emotional learning; the discussion currently is "Can we assess social-emotional learning by using the existing assessment instruments that we currently use for academics? Can multiple choice quizzes, bubble sheets, true-or-false answers, or even essay questions measure and quantify SEL?" And the simple answer is no. You're not going to be able to assess social-emotional development using the same or similar instruments that we currently use. We need to revise the ways that we evaluate and assess students thoroughly. We should start basing assessments on project submissions, rubrics, and group tasks and move away from the standardized testing that we've been doing in this country for over a decade.

III. Forecast for the Future

CASEL has done very well in pushing and advancing the course and cause of social-emotional learning. They've done an excellent job in exposing a large portion of the population of the U.S. to social-emotional learning, and the approaches from CASEL and ASCD's Whole Child approach work together— they are complimentary. So if people go to a school and they're using the work of CASEL, we should examine their approach and results, and if it's working for them, we should say, "Fantastic! Keep doing that if it's working. And here is a whole school framework, and this is where SEL would sit in it. If it makes sense, this might give you additional structure moving forward." Rather than compare and contrast, we should acknowledge that we're all talking about very similar things as part of a bigger movement. Together, we need to continue to have the discussion about what we want our students to gain via our school system. We have to identify and define the characteristics we want as a community and then determine how to know if students have acquired them.

Industry has been telling us again and again that problem-solving, creativity, communication, teamwork, and collaboration are the important 21st-century learning skills that students need, but we currently graduate students who either do or don't possess those skills on a random basis because we don't have the approach in place to reproduce those desirable traits in a formal, systemized education. Most professional organizations are looking for that profile, but those are attributes that are difficult to assess and measure with tests. As educators, we need to carefully define how we wish our graduates to act and behave, and that definition needs to be discussed continually as the needs of industry, community, and society evolve. We need to create a different set of metrics and tools to assess if an individual student or a cohort of students is achieving characteristics of that profile. We must emphasize what we want them to know by the time they leave our system; that allows for a much more mature discussion than just relying on standardized test scores.

Tied back into that, we need to see a change in higher education. Universities and colleges should change the way they do their post-graduation admittance. Many universities and colleges are still using GPA scores and the same basic criteria that they've used for decades to decide who qualifies for freshman admission. But there are positive signs—a growing number of universities and colleges look beyond just the GPA scores and at things that are more telling about a student as a person, such as essays, community service records, and memberships in organizations or clubs. The Harvard Graduate School of Education also recently called for a more holistic, community-centered approach for acceptance into higher education, and their declaration ended up being signed by 200 of the leading universities and colleges around the country.[9] If we continue to see a change there, we will begin to see a more rapid change in the high school system in order to accommodate that approach to admissions.

IV. PATHWAY TO SUCCESS

The very first thing we need to do is discuss a few basic questions: Why do we have an education system? What are we trying to get out of it? What does success look like? That conversation needs to take place at every faculty lounge in every school and in the classrooms of every teacher-training college. These need to be the first questions educators pose to themselves when they become teachers. The answer to that question should be crucial to your personal mission as a teacher, and it should be one of the first questions principals and superintendents ask when they walk into a school. The answer and the conversation it starts needs to take place far more often because they go a long way toward answering many of the questions around social-emotional learning and the outcomes we want from our schools and our kids.

The conversation allows people involved with education to really solidify why they're there and what they're trying to achieve. It doesn't always have to be the same for everyone, but you need to have a reason and rationale for your answer. It also empowers the educators to show they have a role to play in defining the meaning of education beyond just picking up the curriculum from the front office or from the district department and following it word for word. It re-engages stakeholders in the discussion about the education system and demonstrates to them that they can change the conversation on education, helping to shape and craft the discussion and its answers.

Having permission to shape and mold the discussion also allows individual schools and individual districts to develop responses and answers that are correct for their local culture and location. Teachers, educators, and the communities need to feel empowered enough that they feel they can adapt and craft the curriculum to fit the students where they live. The most successful schools that we work with at ASCD all have solid relationships with families, parental cohorts, and local communities. Those schools and districts are the ones that are engaging the community and allowing them to take some control and ownership of what is taking place inside the school.

The missions of CASEL, ASCD, the Aspen Institute, and other SEL-focused organizations all overlap.[10] There is a fairly common agreement among SEL experts that we need to showcase all of the positive work being done with all of the different approaches used in social-emotional learning, including our Whole Child approach, character development, positive school climate, resilience, and grit. You can have more in-depth discussions about what fits inside one or what curriculum works best next to another, but predominantly, they're all talking about the same thing. We all understand that the social-emotional capacities of children need to be developed and that it is crucial schools become adept at the development. We all agree that we need to build skills in teachers so that they can bring these skills out in their students, and we all agree that we need to improve the environment inside the classroom so that teachers have the opportunity to develop the skills.

As long as we are moving in the same direction and see that others are running a similar course, we shouldn't stick to a strict lexicon for SEL. Many of the people in this field have a different term or slightly different definition for the same behavior or technique. A couple of years ago ASCD put out a policy priorities paper by Barbara Michelman called "A Lexicon for Educating the Whole Child (and Preparing the Whole Adult)," which looked at the topic of competing definitions.[11] Competing definitions allow the general public to view all of our work as separate rather than moving in the same direction.

As SEL experts, it is up to all of us to showcase to teachers and education leaders how, in the long run, social-emotional learning will make their lives easier. A lot of the societal issues that are at the forefront of the national discussion at the moment are being unfairly lumped onto teachers. Teachers are overworked, underpaid, under-resourced, and under-respected in our society. They play a critical role in creating good citizens and valued members of our community, but they shouldn't be the only ones that do that. We can help teachers by providing them SEL and the community of support it creates. Plus, many of these teachers are already doing SEL practices, but often without realizing it; they've intuitively taken those difficult first steps toward incorporating SEL into their curriculum without the assistance an SEL approach can provide. Our job as experts in SEL is to find these educators and provide them the approaches they need in order to complete their implementations of SEL purposefully and effectively. In doing so, we improve both the lives and futures of these teachers and their students.

Editor's Reflection Questions

- Where have you missed an opportunity to integrate SEL into other subjects? How can you begin to integrate it?
- Do you believe the definition and purpose of education could exist without addressing students' social-emotional needs? In other words, if schools don't integrate SEL and solely focus on academics and assessment, can they truly say they are delivering a full education?
- Think about the students in your classroom. Describe what you'd want them to be like when they are 25 years old. Is your current curriculum and instruction preparing them for that reality? If not, what must you add?

NOTES

1. If you would like to learn more about our Whole Child approach at ASCD, consult *http://www.ascd.org/whole-child.aspx*.

2. If you would like to learn more about No Child Left Behind, consult *https://www2 .ed.gov/nclb/landing.jhtml*.

3. If you would like to learn more about CASEL, consult *casel.org*.

4. Benjamin Harold, "Chan-Zuckerberg to Push Ambitious New Vision for Personalized Learning," *Education Week*, June 29, 2017, *https://www.edweek.org/ew /articles/2017/06/29/chan-zuckerberg-to-push-ambitious-new-vision-for.html*.

5. If you would like to learn more about ASCD's Whole School, Whole Community, Whole Child model, consult *www.ascd.org/wscc*.

6. If you would like to learn more about the Every Student Succeeds Act, consult *https://www.ed.gov/essa?src=ft*.

7. If you would like to learn more about the Programme for International Assessment administered by the Organization for Economic Co-operation and Development, consult *http://www.oecd.org/pisa/*.

8. If you would like to learn more about the Future of Education and Skills 2030 project, consult *http://www.oecd.org/education/2030/*.

9. Making Caring Common Project, a Project of the Harvard Graduate School of Education, *Turning the Tide: Inspiring Concern for Others and the Common Good through College Admissions*, accessed April 30, 2018, *https://mcc.gse.harvard .edu/files/gse-mcc/files/20160120_mcc_ttt_execsummary_interactive.pdf*.

10. If you would like to learn more about the Aspen Institute, consult *https://www .aspeninstitute.org/*.

11. Barbara Michelman. "A Lexicon for Educating the Whole Child (and Preparing the Whole Adult)." *Policy Priorities* 21, no. 2 (2015): 1-7.

Baruti Kafele

MAKING YOURSELF AN ADVANTAGE FOR YOUR STUDENTS

 **Baruti Kafele** is a best-selling author, keynote speaker, and Milken Award-winning educator who spent nearly 30 years as an urban public school teacher and principal in New Jersey. His books include *Motivating Black Males to Achieve in School and in Life, Closing the Attitude Gap: How to Fire Up Your Students to Strive for Success,* and *The Teacher 50: Critical Questions for Inspiring Classroom Excellence.*

I. CURRENT STATE OF SEL

Social-emotional learning (SEL) was the reason I entered this business in the first place. It was the reason I chose to work where I have. I chose to be in Brooklyn, New York City—in the Crown Heights section right over the subway tracks—because I wanted to respond to social-emotional issues. I felt I had something to offer kids walking in the doors with trauma from home and the streets around us. It wasn't something that came on gradually. I was in the classroom and in a leadership position, and it became my impetus for advancing my career in education.

As schools and districts, our job is to prepare young people for successful lives, so focusing on SEL is not an option—it's a necessity. The same premium that we place on academics, we must place on SEL. There are so many diverse factors to examine. Social-emotional learning is a priority because we need to have a grasp on our emotional status to be a success in life. We've got to have a grip on ourselves socially to work and collaborate with others.

Local

The type and level of SEL depends on where you are in the country. What are your district's demographics and priorities? In Jersey City, New Jersey, the needs of urban kids are enormous. SEL is a priority for us because of the specific needs that young people are bringing into school every day. The needs are overwhelming the academics because there's so much on the students' plates. There's so much that they have to contend with every day of their lives. With a classroom teacher, the primary focus is achievement, but they have many other layers to get through before they can simply focus on the learning.

State

At the state level, the challenges are not equally significant in each place—the higher the poverty level, the more difficult the social-emotional issues tend to be and the more attention lawmakers should pay to them. There is a question that I ask both teachers and various policy leaders about the classroom teachers: "Are your students at an advantage because you teach them?" Immediately, there's a deafening silence in the room. It's a rare day that a teacher or lawmaker wants to answer that question publicly, but they will respond when I let them talk about it amongst themselves. One of the tough questions is how we ensure that any given teacher, school leader, or lawmaker can answer with evidence that their students *are* at an advantage because they're there. And the key is "with evidence."

II. COST OF MAINTAINING THE STATUS QUO

There are many well-intentioned and passionate teachers who want so much for their kids. I meet them every day. But the daily implementation of SEL is where they struggle. If they fail to have the skill and theory to teach their students how to communicate, collaborate, and stay on focus and on task, then they're never going to get to the bottom line of achievement and sustained learning. They're never going to get there because they haven't penetrated the other layers.

As a teacher, you want a student-centered learning environment. You know it's the right way to go, with the focus on the students and their learning. But if the teacher hasn't developed the ability or received the guidance to design an appropriate student-centered learning environment through instilling social skills in the classroom, everything breaks down quickly. Then you are left with 25 to 30 kids in the classroom who cannot work together, who cannot solve problems collaboratively, who cannot interact effectively or in a healthy fashion, and who cannot stay on task together. You not only end up with the students and class off-task, but you also have behavioral problems and discipline challenges, further derailing any learning you had hoped to accomplish.

So you're a superstar in science who knows science inside and out—chemistry, biology, or whatever it might be. You've got some dynamite pedagogical skills. That's fantastic. But we're questioning now how you connect with kids. We're saying that you're a teacher of children first and content second. How do we ensure that we've got teachers in our classrooms that can connect with kids on that level? Because when we connect on that level, the academic achievement will fall in line. In my book *The Teacher 50*, that's the first question I ask.[1] I've led a whole workshop called "Is my school a better school because I lead it?" It looks at the social-emotional side as opposed to the pedagogical side.[2] That's the foundation for success as an educator.

And let me be very clear; I mean teacher with a capital *T*. I'm not suggesting a black teacher with black kids, or a Latino teacher with Latino children. It doesn't equate to knowing those kids. I can come into a classroom full of black kids with a mindset that, because I'm black, I can do it. But just because I'm black doesn't mean I know how to make those connections culturally with young black people. I have to learn their world as well.

III. FORECAST FOR THE FUTURE

If things don't improve, my forecast is bleak. It's a hurricane because teachers don't necessarily know how to teach SEL. There's an important layer of SEL that requires being culturally responsive; it often gets ignored. I'll give you an example.

I don't go to the movies frequently, but because of everything I heard from others, I went to see the film *Black Panther*. I went to see *Selma* in a theater when it was popular, but I did that because I could relate to the real-life civil rights history of *Selma*. I'm not a comic book guy, and I'd never even heard of the Black Panther character. The only one I knew was the Black Panther Party. In fact, when people were initially talking about it, I was thinking that's what it was going to be, but I later realized when it became a phenomenon that it was something else entirely.

I asked people, "What is that?" And they told me. I was on Facebook and Twitter every day, and I saw all the people going into the theater, hyped up and taking pictures next to the cardboard sign, wearing their African attire. I said to my wife, "I have to see this because I've got to understand what's going on here."

But before I even got to the movie, I saw some people on social media complain about the volume of noise in the theater. They complained that people were talking, people were cheering, and people were interacting with the action on the screen. Whereas others were dismayed, as I read that, I understood what was happening because I know the culture. The behavior that people criticized is Baptist church behavior. It's Pentecostal church behavior. It's call-and-response with the pastor throughout the pastor's sermon. It's doing praise and worship while the choir is singing. It's not some quiet, laid-back audience. And then when I got to the theater, it was the same thing. I didn't participate, but I understood it.

The point I'm making is about culture. Someone may see certain behaviors in a setting outside their own culture and think it's not supposed to be that way. But when you're looking at someone else's culture and the behaviors normal to them, you have to take it in *their* context, not your own. You have to take the curriculum to the student because you'll never get the kid to learn the lesson if you drag them to it. My response to what I saw in the movie theater was an example of knowing where I was and who was in the theater. I couldn't be mad at what I was experiencing because I knew that was part of the culture I was immersed in.

Now, imagine being a teacher and seeing aspects of culture that you don't understand from kids. All you know is that you need them to conform to your learning culture because that's your task, your job. You can't reach them because you don't understand them. You may as well be speaking a foreign language that they don't understand. Culturally speaking, you don't know what you're watching or what you're in the midst of, so you end up putting a check-mark on your discipline board because your students aren't in compliance with your rules.

Not understanding the audience that you're working with is the dilemma. It's the challenge. The energies that kids from different cultural backgrounds exhibit can be turned into a positive, but first you've got to learn what it is that you're watching. You learn this by getting to know the children you're working with. You should get to know not just the child, but also their parents and community. As you familiarize yourself, then you understand.

Another example is when I spoke at a program in Wisconsin. A friend of mine was the emcee, and he's a motivational speaker as well. I was ready to talk about Black History Month to three hundred teenagers. It was at a conference with representatives from ten different schools. My friend got them all hyped up with hip-hop music, and I'm sitting there fuming mad, thinking, "I'm coming with a serious black history message, and you are getting these kids too excited."

On the one hand, I'm upset, but on the other hand, I get it. I'm resigned to the fact that I'm going to have to spend a portion of my intro bringing the audience down. But here was the beauty in the moment. The speaker understood his role. He got them excited, but he also realized his role in bringing them down once he finished, and he succeeded in doing that as well. So when I came up to the stage, I was ready to take them back to where they were with my own way instead of music. But here's the point—he and I understood our audience. If you're a teacher, you need to understand your audience. If you don't understand your audience, you're going to have a very tough time establishing an effective learning space.

Since at least 1988, when I started as an educator, there have been a plethora of buzzwords and reform models. Some survive, but most of the models, programs, or activities die out. I think we're on the back end of using the terminology of "mindsets." I do not hear it as frequently, so I think it's peaked. It's not going to disappear because it's important, but when we get beyond language and titles like SEL, mindset, and whatever else we want to use, we can put more emphasis on the substance without necessarily always giving it a label. We can infuse it into the practice.

Trends, by definition, do not have longevity. They're going to die eventually, but they're here for now, and we're hyped by them. Trends in education remind me of fashion. I can't wait for baggy pants to come back. The current trend is skinny pants that I don't like—I don't enjoy the way they fit. But I know they're not going to be here forever. They will be gone, and then the baggy pants I like will come back.

My point is that, when we can go beyond a label or a product itself and put the substance directly into the practice, we're going to produce longevity. Take Madeline Hunter, for instance. Her Instructional Theory in Practice (ITIP) teaching model is no longer widely used, but if you break down how we unfold a lesson, it is still good practice.[3] If we focus just on the practice, there are many classrooms where the ITIP model is not specifically in effect, but some of its basic methods remain—we're just not calling them that anymore. Writing the objective, stating the objective—that process is Madeline Hunter's philosophy. We still do that, but we're not calling it that. If we can ensure that the substance of SEL is infused into our practice, it will stick around and be the game changer we hope it can be.

IV. Pathway to Success

When I first started, everything with me was a theory. I had a lot to learn. Theoretically, I knew that I could meet that need, but I didn't have the practical experience until I got into the classroom. And then, when I saw the divergent needs in the classroom, I knew I had to learn kids from a different vantage point and figure out how I could connect with all of them. I knew that I needed to know kids as more than just their formal teacher. Kids are diverse learners, smart, and occasionally downright brilliant. The kids are extraordinary. But there are too many layers of damage or trauma to contend with and penetrate in order to reach them if we don't understand what we're contending with.

I look at a youngster's attitude toward himself or herself, I look at a youngster's attitude toward school, and I look at a youngster's attitude toward their past or future. How does that kid feel about their own self? It's very easy to get caught up in telling the kid to dream big. Their world is not much wider than their existence. It's a space that's challenging for them to dream in because they don't know that there's a world out there that they can access. They know it exists somewhere, but they don't know if they can put their hands on it.

We're looking at the social-emotional issues in the classroom, but kids are thinking, "Why do I need to conform to your expectations when I don't see the correlation between what you're exposing me to in this classroom and this later-on abstract thing that you're calling 'success'?" And because we can't make that connection or bridge that gap, kids aren't engaged. There's this emotional illusion that there are issues with students when that may not be the case. The suspected and projected problems might not exist, at least not to the extent that they appear to, and our challenge in creating a good learning environment may lie elsewhere.

Years ago, at my last school in Newark, New Jersey, we launched the young men's and young women's empowerment program. We were dealing with the fact that roughly 80% of our students were going home to fatherless households. Mom was playing the dual role of mother and father, putting incredible amounts of pressure on her and the family as a whole. Because of the lack of a father figure, we couldn't be confident that the kids could make the distinction between being young men versus young males, and young women versus young females. Having a father figure in the equation helps make that maturity distinction. To aspire to be something, you have to recognize what it is.

We devised a program mandatory for students as long as they're enrolled in the school. We knew they were facing social-emotional issues. We were going to help them make that distinction between what it is to be an immature male versus a mature man and what it is to be a young female versus a young woman. We were addressing the social-emotional aspects of the youngsters and helping them figure it out.

Using research and our own experiences, we developed the Five Strands, which are five simple questions to help students learn more about themselves, their role in the room with their peers, and their role and responsibilities in the community and society at large. Students in middle school and high school worked around the Five Strands, and we developed them with countless discussions and conversations. We worked with these youngsters with the help of our community partners as well. There were hundreds of people that we tapped throughout the community in Newark to partner with us and to come into the school and work with us on addressing our Five Strands. There are separate Strands for young men and young women; here are the Strands for young men:

Strand 1: What does it look like to be a young man in relationship to himself?

How can any young man get from Point A to Point B in his own personal growth and development socially and emotionally? The average kid will never do it alone if not given the guidance and the direction to get there. This Strand focuses on how to develop a sense of purpose for his life, how to set goals, how to devise a plan, how to have a conversation, how to listen when another person is talking, and how to demonstrate respect for your fellow men. What does the grind of getting from Point A to Point B look like professionally or in personal progress? What are reasonable and challenging goals to set along the way? When they've got a tough situation and reach a roadblock or an obstacle, how do they respond to it? How do they react to it emotionally?

And we had all of these parts of the conversation while we were also raising average test scores that started in that school in the high 20s in mathematics and the low 30s in language arts. We had these academic challenges, but we knew we had to deal with this other aspect first, and we figured that, if done successfully, this aspect would pull the academics up along with it. And it did.

Strand 2: What does it look like to be a young man in relationship to the young ladies in the building?

There are issues related to the respect and appreciation for young ladies found in pop culture, music, and societal norms. All these variables essentially translate into the young man in our society not holding the young lady up on a pedestal. That's one of the main issues we spent time working with them on—teaching them that everyone deserves respect.

Strand 3: What does it look like to be a young man in relationship to the child he may or may not have?

How can a young man genuinely understand his role as a father if he's never seen a role model in action? There was a considerable volume of young men who could not intellectually project into what fatherhood might look like because they were too deep into their current reality of "I'm not happy with my situation because I don't have access to my own father." A kid would often express this, or he would express hatred for his father. That rage might come out in a conversation in the cafeteria.

So we would say to him, "If that's how you feel based on your current reality, how will your own child feel 10 years or 15 years from now when they reflect on you?" We were instilling that philosophy and point of view; we were planting that seed while the kid was still sitting in grade school.

Strand 4: What does it look like to be a young man in relationship to his male peers?

A lot of urban schools have a gang problem, whether they want to own up to it or not. We had a gang infestation in Newark, just as we do in many places that I visit. Anything can rub the wrong way in those schools because you've got gangs in those classrooms. Tensions can be very high. It doesn't take much to have an issue.

But what if, in the conversation with young men, we can convince them that what binds them together as young men is stronger than those artificial gang colors that separate them? That's the angle that we have used and continue to use to build unity amongst young men, and it works. The young men have unified across racial and ethnic lines. Prior gang affiliation was not a deterrent to these young men being able to demonstrate their brilliance, collaborate on projects, and coexist in the same space.

The youngster can demonstrate his brilliance because of the climate and culture created. We give them the safe space, the self-esteem, and the confidence to be as smart and as creative as they want to be. They often say, "I can be who I am. I've got a certain reputation as a gang member, but I can come into this space and demonstrate that I'm brilliant and not suffer social consequences as a result."

Strand 5: What does it look like to be a young man in relationship to his community?

Our goal is to have the student ask, "Am I a liability to my community, or am I an asset? Am I a source of strength and support to the community in which I live?" Young men will often leave my meetings hyped up; they are ready to be mature and responsible men. The young ladies are very similar. It just happens that, when we're talking with young ladies, their needs are different. The outcome of each meeting is entirely different, especially when we're talking with urban young ladies about what they have to handle. The reality is different, so the outcomes of the meetings are different. But we still get the results we need.

In Newark, we would take our senior class and tell them, "You're responsible for leading your younger peers." We taught these kids not only leadership, but also oratory skills. We taught them how to speak publicly in front of their peers and community. In their senior year, they became the co-principals, responsible for constantly talking to the freshman class in a very structured setting and reminding them of the expectations for them as they move forward. Then they went into the elementary schools and did the same thing. We had a whole class of seniors helping build a bridge across elementary school, middle school, and high school.

Socially and emotionally, kids are transforming right before our eyes. We're watching them go through a metamorphosis because they're grappling head-on with the issues we're putting in their faces. Their achievement levels are rising because the youngsters have a purpose for being in the classroom in the first place.

Remember that question I told you about, the question that I ask about classroom teachers: "Are your students at an advantage because you teach them?" I don't stop there. If teachers answer yes, I ask, "Why so? What puts that kid at an advantage with you in the space?" I break down the question not because the teacher may come in with superior pedagogical skills, but instead because I wish to know if kids are at an advantage because of emotional connections. Has the teacher made those connections? Because when the students are engaged, they can learn anything, and that's the ultimate goal of social-emotional learning in the classroom.

Editor's Reflection Questions

- Do you believe your students are at an advantage because you are their teacher? Why or why not?
- When is the last time you had a misconception about a student or group of students that you had to intentionally confront and correct? How did you face it and how did you make the correction?
- In what ways do you connect to your students' interests, backgrounds, and cultures?

NOTES

1. Baruti Kafele. *The Teacher 50: Critical Questions for Inspiring Classroom Excellence.* (Alexandria: ASCD, 2017).

2. More information about this workshop and the lessons it teaches can be found in "Is Your School Better Because You Lead It?" *Lifting School Leaders* 74, no. 8 (2017): 10-14.

3. For more information about Madeline Hunter's ITIP lesson plan model, check out *https://thesecondprinciple.com/teaching-essentials/models-of-teaching/madeline-hunter-lesson-plan-model/.*

Peter DeWitt

CREATING AN INCLUSIVE SCHOOL CLIMATE

Peter DeWitt, EdD, is a former K–5 teacher (11 years) and principal (8 years). He runs workshops and provides keynotes nationally and internationally focusing on collaborative leadership, fostering inclusive school climates, and connected learning. Within North America, his work has been adopted at the state and university levels, and he works with numerous districts and school boards.

I. CURRENT STATE OF SEL

Social-emotional learning (SEL) varies according to where and when it is being implemented. Many district and state leaders say it's important, but don't know how to fit SEL into all their other responsibilities. Where does SEL fit in academic learning? How does it fit into their mandates, the curriculum, and the pedagogy? How does it fit into the classrooms and corridors on a daily basis? For me, social-emotional learning happens with authentic student engagement—when kids lean in, ask questions more than just being put in the position of answering them, and have a voice in their own learning.

For some leaders, SEL is a good talking point, but they don't do anything about it, even though there are experts and programs the district can contract with to come into the schools, do the climate work, and lay out the ground-work to actually make it easier for them.

Beyond just being aware of SEL, schools must recognize the fact that it should be—and can easily be—a part of everyday conversations. It's as simple as how you talk to students in the hallway. Do we jump to a conclusion before we talk to them? Do we instantly yell at them for not having a pass? Do we assume that they are in trouble because it's during class time that we see them "wandering"? Or do we simply ask them how their day is going and wait to see what they tell us? Can we possibly find more empathetic ways to engage with all of our students, even the ones who may be having a rough day?

Shaun Harper of the University of Pennsylvania says that we refer to groups as a minority, but the reality is they're not a minority within family or friendship groups.[1] Sometimes, they're not even a minority within the population. They are actually minoritized by others. Indigenous populations have been minoritized globally, and the same is true for many other groups.

People are not oblivious. Everyone can see what's going on around us, whether it's elections or school shootings or kids suffering from trauma. If you're in the education community and see the research, you can't deny it anymore. For SEL to combat these issues successfully, people need awareness of what it is. Social-emotional learning is not only reframing the adult-learner relationship. It's also reframing and redefining leadership. We have to change the basic mindset of what a leader is. There's still so much of a disconnect between how teachers are being trained in higher education and what they're prepared for when they walk into a classroom. We as educators need to come together and support each other and the next generation of teachers.

II. Cost of Maintaining the Status Quo

We have many issues that need to be solved in this country. Unfortunately, too often it's easier to yell our opinions than it is to gain an understanding of those we are talking to. One area where schools get pushback is SEL, but we cannot view SEL as an extra or an add-on. SEL is as important as academic learning, and it's desperately needed. It may help us break from the cycle of yelling at each other and create a space where we actually listen and learn from each other.

In today's society, the news is full of stories of people arguing over the inconsequential things. Wouldn't we want people to be able to talk those things out, understand where other people are coming from, and be able to have dialogue? Social-emotional learning helps develop those skills in kids. With its message of inclusion and respect, social-emotional learning is a positive thing we should be talking about.

In a diverse classroom, teachers should be sensitive to the simple fact that many of their students, based upon their experiences and the context that they bring into the classroom from their life outside the school walls, might disagree with a teacher's conclusions. Teaching controversial topics doesn't mean that all students have to agree with the perception of the teacher. Teaching controversial topics means that teachers and students discuss topics and respect each other's diverse views. Educators must model how to discuss differences and disagreements respectfully—that's how meaningful relationships get started.

We know that relationships matter. Education researcher John Hattie looked at student-teacher relationships and determined that they have a very high effect on kids.[2] Zero tolerance policies and expulsions just isolate kids from their community and detach them from the very relationships and resources they desperately need. Social-emotional learning is like having an early warning system that allows us to see what kind of behaviors are sticking out and helps us figure out a better way to help kids before it's too late. But the relationship shouldn't be a reactive approach; it should be a proactive approach. The relationship is the social-emotional learning.

III. FORECAST FOR THE FUTURE

There are people who don't think social-emotional learning has a place in school because they believe the focus needs to be on academics. But everything is a puzzle, and it only fits together if you do it right. Because of how trauma affects the learning environment, the academic piece will never fully fit in the puzzle if you don't have the social-emotional learning piece.

A Center for Disease Control (CDC) report released in 2013 estimated that 13–20% of children in the United States "experience a mental disorder in a given year."[3] Additionally, a survey conducted with over 10,000 teens by Kathleen Merikangas of the National Institute for Mental Health (NIMH) found that only 36% of the respondents who had ever experienced a mental health disorder had actually received any treatment.[4] That is a huge red flag. We have kids who are coming into the building from terrible situations at home, and the school climate might be their sanctuaries. Their teachers might be the only beacons of light they have throughout their day. So SEL is not an add-on; it's the plate that everything else gets served on.

Schools need to invest in an early warning system that focuses on the academic and social-emotional needs of students. An early warning system takes note of the typical things like tardy marks, absences, and daily operational data, but it also looks at family engagement—how involved are the parents? It has progress monitoring and curriculum-based measures, but it also looks at teacher engagement. These conversations around early warning systems take place in child study teams or on department levels, and they need to shift from trying to figure out what's wrong with the child to determining the strategies that can be used to engage the student in the classroom and empower them when they're engaged.

The climate of leadership is also very much a part of SEL. Besides the assistant principal, the most important leaders in the building are the school counselor and school psychologist. They need to meet every week and talk about kids who are "on the radar." On the classroom level, teachers need to have time to have the spreadsheet in front of them so they can put information into it and see which kids are starting to come to the top and which kids need more attention. The information should reveal any kid who might otherwise be hidden, but there shouldn't be so much information that it is overwhelming to the teacher. It's a fine line that varies from teacher to teacher.

IV. Pathway to Success

We need to make SEL implementation as simple as we can by using simple language and uncomplicated ideas. Here are six enabling conditions that need to be in place for social-emotional learning to take root and flourish:

1. School board policy

It is important that the school board sets policies such as codes of conduct. Leaders need codes of conduct covering the entire school day to support any decision that they put in place. For example, New York has the Dignity for All Students Act.[5] This law requires curriculum to discuss a lot of different populations and cultures, so educators are supported by a strong code of conduct if parents object.

2. Images in hallways

As strange as this sounds, images in the hallways are an essential part of creating the correct culture and atmosphere in the school. When pictures are up in the hallways that do not necessarily reflect the diversity in the classroom, children don't feel welcome in the school. If there are pictures up on the walls of the corridor that don't represent the identities of the student population walking through them, the images affect the students on a deep level. On the other hand, art and posters in the hallways and classrooms that celebrate diversity and inclusion can make a student that would otherwise feel marginalized and isolated feel welcomed and included. And for the people who ask, "Are images in hallways really important?"—if images weren't important, then Facebook and Instagram wouldn't be popular.

3. Representative curriculum

Is your curriculum inclusive? Are minority populations represented in the curriculum? In your lessons, do you teach by holding classroom debates and freewheeling discussions? Can your students talk about anything from economic disparity to race issues that we're dealing with in America? Or when these topics come up, are they often treated with avoidance, marginalization, and blame that sends negative messages to these populations? Curriculum is very important, and the context that goes along with it is significant as well.

Ultimately, teachers and administrators need to avoid suggesting that students are "bad" when they don't agree with them about issues. If students are taught something but still don't agree with it, they are often vilified for not accepting, but they don't need to be on board. Instead, they need to be able to have a dialogue and to be okay with each other. That's a big part of what social-emotional learning is all about—agreeing to disagree and still being able to work and play with each other. Everyone doesn't have to accept everything that is being talked about. It certainly doesn't mean they're bad people because they believe something else. They just need to listen and respect the other person in the conversation.

4.   *Inclusive books and novels in your library*

It's very important that, when a student walks into the school library, they see minority populations truly and positively represented in the books and magazines available to them. We know that, for a long time, Native Americans were not portrayed positively in our history books, and the damage done to their culture throughout history is still being dealt with and felt. The negative depictions of minorities in old Hollywood movies and television sitcoms promoted negative stereotypes, but positive and inclusive art can help dispel the myths created by those generations of bigotry and prejudice.

5.   *Common language*

Common language is really important for school climate. It's necessary for people to know what language to use. When you walk into a school and hear teachers and administrators using the same acronyms and terms to make sure everyone is on the same page and heading in the same direction, that's powerful. Communication is critical, and a common language is a huge element of effective communication.

6. *Professional development*

Training by professionals who understand the context of schools is imperative. If you are not the expert, don't act like you're the expert. Find who the expert is and have a conversation with them. It is their job to tell you where to start and how to be prepared. Make sure that the organizations that you're working with completely understand your context and they're not just coming in to give you a package deal. Unfortunately, some organizations like to come in and push their agenda even though they're several steps ahead of the school they're trying to help. Because of time and budget restraints, these organizations just say, "Don't worry, you'll catch on," and end up with a severe communication gap.

That can be very detrimental to the school moving forward because the organization is talking about its concepts and ideas in a language that the people in the school don't understand. When the agency leaves once their contract ends, the teachers aren't going to change anything. They'll just keep doing what hasn't been working for them or their students up until then. An anonymous pre-engagement survey should be sent out so the staff can write down what they wish the administration or SEL team knew about them. It helps build a bridge of communication and empathy better than just dumping a new curriculum on the staff and telling them that they're not doing enough to learn it as individuals or a group.

Editor's Reflection Questions

- Think about your school or the last school you've entered. How would you describe the way the entrance, hallways, offices, and classrooms look and feel? If you had to classify the school climate as positive or negative, which way would you lean?
- What are one or two ways your school's climate could be more inclusive? Where have you missed opportunities to reach out to marginalized populations?
- What are the must-have terms and definitions you'd include on a list of common language for your school, district, or organization?

NOTES

DeWitt, Peter. *Collaborative Leadership: 6 Influences That Matter Most.* (Thousand Oaks, CA: Corwin Press, 2016).

DeWitt, Peter. *School Climate: Leading With Collective Efficacy.* (Thousand Oaks, CA: Corwin Press, 2017).

1. Shaun R. Harper. "Race without Racism: How Higher Education Researchers Minimize Racist Institutional Norms." *The Review of Higher Education* 36, no. 1 (2012): 9–29.

2. John Hattie. *Visible Learning for Teachers: Maximizing Impact on Learning.* (London: Routledge, 2012).

3. CDC. "Mental Health Surveillance Among Children — United States, 2005–2011." Supplement, *Morbidity and Mortality Weekly Report* 62, no. 2 (May 17, 2013): 1-35.

4. Kathleen Ries Merikangas, Jian-ping He, Marcy P. Burstein, Joel Swendsen, Shelli Avenevoli, Brady Case, Katholiki Georgiades, Leanne Heaton, Sonja Swanson, Mark Olfson. "Service utilization for lifetime mental disorders in U.S. adolescents: Results from the National Comorbidity Survey Adolescent Supplement (NCS-A)." *Journal of the American Academy of Child and Adolescent Psychiatry* 50, no. 1 (2011): 32-45.

5. Check *http://www.p12.nysed.gov/dignityact/* to learn more about New York State's Dignity for All Students Act.

Tara Subramaniam

AMPLIFYING STUDENT VOICE FOR IMPACT

Tara Subramaniam co-founded Student Voice in the summer of 2012 with a vision of creating a place where all students could share their ideas. Before becoming Executive Director, she previously served as Director of Programming where she managed the organization's cornerstone Twitter chats. She is currently studying at Georgetown's Walsh School of Foreign Service. Tara loves to write, read, run, travel, and learn new languages.

I. CURRENT STATE OF SEL

The local and regional statuses of social-emotional learning (SEL) are diverse across the entire country, so it's hard to sum up the overall status of SEL. There are pockets that are doing well, and there are areas that are really struggling. Overall, I do believe there is a growing emphasis on school climate nationwide. People are having conversations about how students are feeling in schools. That's really exciting, but we must make sure to involve students in these conversations. How can we discuss school climate without asking students how they're feeling? If we don't ask them, we're just throwing ideas out there and hoping that we guess right. We can hope they'll say, "Yes, you guessed exactly what I'm feeling," but there's no guarantee that will happen.

Local
Districts and schools are being more cognizant of the impact of digital technology on students' social-emotional wellness. They are expanding

the scope and realizing that, even when students are not in classrooms, the things they do outside of their school walls impact their learning performance and brain function. Schools have to create an environment and a culture where students feel comfortable sharing when they have a problem, a place where the relationships between students and staff are safe, healthy, and productive within the school and the classroom.

Districts are addressing issues like cyberbullying, which wasn't an issue when people started talking about social-emotional learning. Traditionally, when you think about problems within the school, you think about the bully on the schoolyard, but that's not what it looks like anymore. On apps and other anonymous forums, kids really want to hear what their peers think about them and therefore open themselves up to criticism and abuse by the people that seize the opportunity and misuse that power.

The mission for districts and schools is to create a school environment where students feel comfortable sharing with teachers and staff—a place where students will not feel scared that what they say in person or on social media will come back to hurt them.

The answer to this one simple question is an alert to the state of a school's social-emotional learning environment: Do students have a voice? In other words, are students being given the opportunities to share their perspectives? Are they being listened to? Are their ideas being put into action? We've made a lot of progress; schools are allowing students more and more opportunities to speak up in small ways. In the past, schools would send out a simple survey and pat themselves on the back and say, "Great! Whatever the survey results are, we've gotten student input." But there was never enough student turnout to influence the decisions, and students would become frustrated because their input wasn't really making an impact. The important part of engaging students is the follow-up, the execution. It's all about creating the opportunity for the students to have meaningful input and then actually acting upon whatever is revealed.

If there is an open-door policy, focus group, or advisory council where students are involved in the process, the superintendent will realize that there's progress to be made. But if discussions about SEL needs are happening with just the adults, you're missing something crucial in the data. You are making decisions that affect the day-to-day lives of these students and can impact their future, their entire trajectory, without authentic awareness or knowledge of what the students really need. It's impossible to ignore the fact that what happens to students in high school has a weighty impact over the course of their lifetimes. It is possible for them to deviate from the course that gets set in high school, but it often really sets the tone for the rest of their lives. When decisions to impact those environments are being made without including the students, there's a big and influential gap in the results.

The Digital Realm

Student Voice—the student-run education nonprofit I cofounded back in 2012—started as a Twitter chat.[1] It was created out of the desire to bring students into the conversations happening about education. When Student Voice was founded, teachers were a large population of people on Twitter, so we decided that it should be our entry point. We wanted to inject the student perspective and be a part of those conversations that educators were having.

Student Voice started the hashtag #StuVoice and held a weekly Twitter chat every Monday at 8:30 p.m. ET for four years. Different guests each week would talk about various issues that were important to students. We brought in Frank Bruni from the *New York Times* during the college application season, and we facilitated a discussion about college acceptance.[2] Students needed to hear that maybe it's not the biggest deal if you don't get into that Ivy League school you've been dreaming about all your life. For some students, this was a major source of stress, and it was a relief to be told this.

Twitter allowed us to create an even playing field because, on Twitter, it doesn't matter if you are the tallest or loudest person in the room. If you have something to say, you can say it, and it will be heard. It helped drive the conversations about what students wanted to be talking about and helped students engage various stakeholders on these issues. That's one of the things that was powerful about the platform and helped drive the message home.

Students will still often say, "This is great. Thank you for sharing our voices." But for change to happen it takes a movement; it takes a lot of partnerships in the school, the district, and the community. The major changes start happening when teachers indicate they actually care about what students have to say, start to listen, begin responding, and help.

Advocacy

Educators also need to be advocates for their students, especially in situations where students aren't given the opportunity to speak for themselves. When teachers and staff head into meetings with lawmakers and policymakers where students can't be present, they should make an effort to meet with them beforehand and say, "Give me your ideas. I want to hear what you're saying so I am informed when I go to this meeting. I can have the weight of your perspectives behind what I'm saying so that I'm not just spouting things. I'm going to represent you, and I'm going to do what I can to make sure that your perspectives are heard." There's a very structured system already in place, and breaking it down is going to be a long process. Some states are trying to create an educational culture where everybody feels included and welcome, but so far they are few and far between.

A lot of professors and administrators do a good job before testifying of getting people to write down quotes so that they're not paraphrasing. They have literal evidence that they can show. I've seen school board meetings where students gave written testimony to a member to read aloud because students weren't allowed to testify. The ultimate goal is always to create more inclusion and more opportunities for students to have a voice in their learning.

II. Cost of Maintaining the Status Quo

Social-emotional learning is very nuanced. Bullying is a big issue affecting the learning environment, and it goes deeper and encompasses a lot more than what most people think. For example, a problem for many students in high school is eating disorders, an issue that seems to cross both cultural and economic lines across the country. Many times it's not a direct result of blatant bullying, but instead a result of when you hang out with the cool people. They are buying clothes, and you can't buy those clothes. They are eating this, and you can't eat that. It is bullying, but it's very subtle and nuanced. To say that just one or two underlying issues are affecting social-emotional learning is ignoring a lot of the ways that small daily interactions between students have an impact in a significant way.

Social-emotional learning can help improve the daily conversation between students in the hallway. You see these campaigns that say a smile can change somebody's day, and it's so true. If somebody is having a bad day, a stranger taking the time to say, "Oh, you look so put together today!" or "Hey, do you want this coffee?" or "I'm done; do you want my seat?" can make a huge difference. Students and staff can do little things like chalk positive messages in their quad or along the steps or put little notes in the bathroom stalls that say positive things. If you've had a bad day, it's pouring rain, and you just had an exam, someone telling you to have a nice day might not really do anything to change your luck, but it will make you laugh or, at the very least, smile. And that smile will send messages to your brain that say, "Okay, this is a positive thing. I'm not as sad as I was five minutes ago."

Little things like that—the really little things that don't take much effort—can have a massive impact on school climate. They can make a huge difference to someone. Small things can make a big difference on both ends of the interaction, and that is a component of SEL that gets overlooked far too often. Many social-emotional learning campaigns try to tackle the significant problems, but people don't realize that a lot of good comes out of the small things.

III. Forecast for the Future

For social-emotional learning to take root, there needs to be a cultural shift. The best way to ensure an authentic response is to ask the students, not just a group of staff, administrators, and the superintendent. Some universities are doing a really good job sending out regular surveys to gauge the health and wellness habits of their students by asking pertinent questions like "How much sleep do you get? How many meals do you eat? How many times do you exercise? How many times do you leave campus? How many times do you go out? How many times have you felt safe?" They use these statistics and put them up on campus in really engaging and interesting ways.

But it's not publicized how many people actually participated in the survey and how the gathered data was vetted. If you ask students, you need to do it in such a way that you know people honestly participated. Otherwise, you'll be using incomplete data, leaving you unsure if you can or cannot trust the results. Additionally, are students being asked to create the questions? Are the markers misleading?

Multiple-choice questions like "I go out: none; a little; not much; sometimes; a lot" become very nebulous, and sometimes students are presented with vague and nonspecific ranges like "I get somewhere between six to ten hours of sleep." That's a large gap in the data, and it makes a big difference not only in the results, but in the analysis of the data as well. If the results say that 50% of students get six to ten hours of sleep, are most of them getting closer to just six hours of sleep? The way the question is asked skews the results.

If a school doesn't have a study to measure how people are feeling, then a survey is a great first step. If people don't want to fill out surveys, host roundtable discussions. At Student Voice, we've received a lot of good feedback hosting roundtables. Professors will listen to the recordings of our podcast where students are comfortable sharing what they feel, and they are amazed. If you ask students direct questions, they have a lot to say, so learning to ask the right questions to get honest answers is very important.

If you are conducting an audit on the state of a school's social-emotional well-being, take it even another step further and involve students in the audit. Don't just include them in the initial planning, but keep them involved in every step. Continue to check in with the students throughout the process. Even under the best of circumstances, it's almost mathematically impossible for a superintendent to speak to every student, so either have a student representative on the school board or create a student superintendent's advisory council. Depending on how it's structured, it can be a powerful tool. If the student advisory council is application-based and recommendation-based, though, it has some limits.

Overall, there's only progress to be made from here, and there are a lot of reasons for optimism. Looking at current events, the momentum of support for students is increasing. President Barack Obama responded to the incredible activism of the Parkland students by essentially saying that we should listen to students because they know what they're doing.[3] This is the kind of public attitude that I didn't see in high school when I was growing up. The standard response was always "Sure, you have a voice, but do you really know what you're talking about? Are you sure we should listen to you?"

Students today are showing that they have an immense passion for the issues that they're working on. They are working from a place of genuine concern. It's not that they're co-opting issues that they read about in the news. This is happening in their backyard, and they know it needs to stop. That sense of student ownership is driving student advocacy and bodes well for student empowerment and social-emotional learning moving forward.

IV. Pathway to Success

After Student Voice officially became incorporated as a nonprofit, we began visiting students across the country through conferences and continued talking with them through the Twitter chats. We launched a national tour where we would visit students and host roundtables. We found from the conferences, the Twitter chats, and the roundtables that students felt the education system in general was not meeting their basic fundamental rights as students. These conversations inspired the Student Bill of Rights, an online platform where students could identify the issues that affected them within their schools.

The benefit of the Student Bill of Rights is that it's a broad enough framework that many issues and problems are addressed. The right to free expression, the right to due process, the right to technology, the right to a positive school climate, the right to diversity and inclusivity—we believe that these are fundamental rights that students should have in the American education system. The Student Bill of Rights helps students who want to become more involved in their schools and take charge of their education identify where their community needs the most help. Education is not one size fits all; there are a variety of issues impacting the education system across the country. These are the nine individual pillars of the Student Bill of Rights:

1. *Access and Affordability:* All students have the right to an affordable and equitable education.

2. *Civic Participation:* All students have the right to expect that they as citizens and their schools as institutions are engaged with the broader community.

3. *Influence Decisions:* All students have the right to shape and understand the institutions that will affect their academic futures.

4. *Diversity and Inclusion:* All students have the right to learn in an environment that doesn't discriminate against them for who they are and reflects the variety of backgrounds in the student body.

5. *Modern Technology:* All students have the right to learn in a space where modern technology is actively incorporated.

6. *Deeper Learning:* All students have the right to an education that prepares them for their lives beyond school by tailoring to their individual needs.

7. *Due Process:* All students have the right to understand the rules and procedures in their schools and to be provided with opportunities to address unfair treatment.

8. *Free Expression*: All students have the right to express themselves within an educational context to the extent that said expression causes no harm.

9. *Positive School Climate*: All students have the right to feel mentally, physically, and emotionally safe in school.

The nine individual pillars all interact and lean on each other, and together, they strongly affect social-emotional learning. Access and Affordability, for example, is the concept that all students deserve access to quality education that doesn't break the bank or require them to work two jobs. If education negatively impacts their family budgets, students feel guilty, and if they're juggling multiple responsibilities and must focus on one of those other responsibilities, they often have to miss school. On the other hand, if you have a system that is both accessible and affordable, you have students who are happier in school and who feel less ostracized and less stressed because they have fewer external pressures that impact their learning. It's an example of how that pillar alone affects social-emotional learning.

Diversity and Inclusion is a right that's intrinsically tied to Positive School Climate—they go hand in hand. When people feel included in a positive environment, they feel better about the community, and they are willing to give back. They are eager to work harder, and they can concentrate more. In middle school, when students don't feel like they fit in or don't feel like people are listening, they start to withdraw and lose a lot of the benefits that a healthy learning environment has to offer, even though they are present in the room. Again, the ultimate goal is always to create more inclusion and more opportunities for students to have a voice in their learning and their future.

Editor's Reflection Questions

- How do we move from the place where including student voice is an *exception* to a place where it is an *expectation*?
- What are one or two things you've learned from listening to students that you wouldn't have otherwise realized? How did this help you better address students' pressing needs?
- How much do you know about the specific social-emotional needs created by the digital world, including those caused by cyberbullying or simply from the "second screen," "always-on" experience of digital natives? What are some gaps in your knowledge you can address by creating a better platform for student voice?

NOTES

1. See *https://www.stuvoice.org/* for more information about Student Voice.

2. See *https://www.nytimes.com/by/frank-bruni* for information about Bruni and access to the articles he's written on education and a variety of other subjects for the *New York Times*.

3. Barack Obama, Twitter Post, February 22, 2018, 8:00 a.m. *https://twitter.com /BarackObama/status/966704319658647553*

Richard Gerver

HELPING KIDS TURN DREAMS INTO ASPIRATIONS

Richard Gerver is a former teacher and school leader who authored the best-selling books *Creating Tomorrow's Schools Today, Change,* and *Simple Thinking.* He is an internationally recognized and celebrated speaker whose insights into change and leadership have opened doors to work with organizations such as Google, Harrods, and Deloitte. He has also had the privilege to keynote education conferences, advise a presidential campaign, and support worldwide Olympic sports organizations.

I. CURRENT STATE OF SEL

The world our kids are growing up in is, without a doubt, the most complex era ever known in the human experience. From increasing technology and globalization to issues around environment and economy, kids have never grown up in a more uncertain time. That's partly exacerbated by the prevalence and availability of inexpensive technology and by the attitudes held by some adults about kids.

In the United Kingdom, adults talk about "snowflake culture." They use this phrase to suggest that our kids are somehow less strong, committed, dynamic, and resilient than their forebears. I also detect this same attitude in the United States, and in both locations, it is a real issue that kids have with their parents and other adults in their lives.

Our Global Society

When I was growing up, I was gloriously unaware of the real challenges facing society. I knew about the Cold War because every so often there would be a television advertisement telling us what to do in case of a nuclear attack, but I had no idea how close we were to a nuclear war. I didn't understand the ramifications. I didn't know what issues were sparking conflicts around the world. I wouldn't have known about a terrorist attack in the U.S. I wouldn't have known about the rise of extremists in Germany. I wouldn't have known about those things because I was a child living in the cocoon of an overprotective family without easy access to news. Kids of today have that access.

Modern kids are more aware than we ever were, like it or not. Part of the problem is that they're aware of the horrific and dynamic events happening right in front of them on social media and the internet but not mature enough to process them. No one is talking to them about this stuff. The kids are aware of it but aren't mature enough to deal with the issues raised. They are unable to process the emotions and concepts put before them logically and confidently.

We're living in a high-stakes society where the future is less certain than it's ever been; this uncertainty creates a huge vacuum that drives a lot of the issues around social-emotional well-being in our kids. After all, educational theory was built for over a millennium on searching for certainty in the world around us. The education system in its traditional form has always been predicated on formulas: "Do this, and this will happen; do that, and that will happen. Pass this test, and this will happen; go to college, and that will happen." Nothing is certain anymore in today's world.

We've been trained from age seven or eight to work in an industrial world. We and our forebears were taught that, if we sought out jobs, became indispensable and technically proficient in those jobs, and did what we're told, we would be given jobs for life, livable wages, and pensions, no matter if we were blue or white collar. The system is based on certainty, and in the U.K. and the U.S., we are still trying to re-create that certainty in education, but that world of certainty has changed around us.

Kids in the U.K. today are among the most tested in the world. Nick Gibb, the National Schools Minister in the U.K. (the equivalent of the U.S. Secretary of Education), recently announced a new battery of tests for eight-year-olds, and his justification was because mental health in British schools is a big issue. He said the reason we're bringing in more tests is that it will actually make kids more emotionally resilient: the more tests they have, the stronger they become and the fewer mental health problems there will be.[1]

In other words, we're in the midst of a very interesting clash of ideologies and philosophies right now. We have a generation that believes that kids are "snowflakes" and need to toughen up, and there's no reason for them to feel vulnerable or emotionally trapped. These people say there's no place for social-emotional learning in our schools because it gets in the way of the "proper" stuff, the "traditional" education.

Because of this attitude, countries like the U.K. and the U.S. are heavily focused on the academic outcomes of standardized tests, but we honestly haven't got time for this. The Programme for International Student Assessment (PISA) and the over-testing it encourages are clouding the national educational agenda.[2]

II. Cost of Maintaining the Status Quo

I was first conscious of social-emotional learning (SEL) without knowing it was called by that name. I came from a very middle-class background, as many teachers do, and first started teaching in the U.K. in a school that was in an area of terrible social deprivation. I had been trained to deliver a standard curriculum, and I was prepared well to do it. I remember realizing in the first couple of weeks of being in that school that there were nine-year-old children in my class who were living in the most horrific conditions at home and bringing that trauma to school with them. There were kids whose fathers were in prison for murder. There were kids whose mothers were prostituting themselves to feed a drug habit. There were kids who were living with five or six brothers and sisters, all with different parents. There were kids in foster care. There were kids for whom it was a miracle to just be there in the morning, much less in a fit state to learn.

I was trained very early on as a young teacher to apply the same rules, training, and systems I'd been taught in college across all economic and cultural borders and believe that everyone could understand the British middle-class set of values and principles. But I learned very quickly that, if I wanted my kids to develop in any way intellectually and academically, there was no point in feeding them that stuff until I'd helped them become emotionally safe in my classroom. They needed to understand the educational process, the events happening in the world around them, and the impacts those events were having in their own lives. Having had a tiny grain of that as a child going through the very messy divorce of my parents, I had an emotional connection.

There is now a real recognition and understanding that if kids don't feel safe, secure, adjusted, loved, and respected in the classroom, they will never learn effectively. Unless students believe that there are people there who will listen to their voice and understand their issues to help them in a more three-dimensional way, they're never going to learn, no matter how hard you drive stuff at them or punish them if they don't achieve.

Meanwhile, our kids are being exposed to the uncertainty of life and are aware of its fragility. They're aware that the world isn't a safe, happy, and certain place. They see that the opportunities to advance and flourish in the way like their parents and grandparents did are fewer and farther between in today's economy.

Let's use my home area in the East Midlands as a metaphor for education. First, here's a little history. If you take Scotland off the top of the map of England, the East Midlands are literally in the middle of the country. The two main cities—Derby and Nottingham—are mid-sized cities in British terms and are both fiercely competitive, independent cities with history around mining, textiles, and furniture design. In other words, big factories exist. In fact, Derby is the home to the world's first commercial factory. The Industrial

Age began in the East Midlands, which provides an important context to help understand the region.

Long Eaton is a town on the border of both cities and also a town that, throughout history, has had periods of huge affluence. It was at the heart of the Industrial Age, particularly around textile manufacturing and mining. It's an intensely independent town, and the people in Long Eaton don't consider themselves Derby or Nottingham. They fiercely believe themselves Long Eaton, and it's a very insular community as a result of this mindset. Unless you were born in Long Eaton, you will never be a local of Long Eaton. You could have lived there thirty years, but if you weren't born there, you're not a Long Eaton person and never will be.

Over time, as the primary industries moved out—the textile market moved to Asia, coal mining was closed down—all the various commercial industries that popped up over the centuries to support the industrial base and its employees went away, and the economy slowly collapsed. It went from being a relatively affluent community to being an incredibly socially deprived community because all the industries left but the people didn't.

Long Eaton maintained its fierce autonomy. They're still protective and insular. The problem is that it actually leads to a self-perpetuating absence of hope and aspiration. Over the last fifty or sixty years, that vacuum of lack of business and industry has sucked the hope out of the community. In Long Eaton, if you get a job in the local supermarket like Mom or Grandma has, that's the absolute best you're going to do. That's as good an opportunity as there is going to be.

As a result, they don't accept strangers very well in Long Eaton. What's interesting about the increased insularity of Long Eaton—and what I think is also true about the increased insularity of the education profession today—is that, when you're on the edge of failure, when you're threatened, when things are going badly, you tend to close in on yourselves. You tend to become very bunkered in mentally, very hunkered down.

We see it in so many aspects of society today, possibly as a result of the financial crises in 2007 and 2008. It's no coincidence that we're seeing major global powers like the United States and the United Kingdom become more and more insular and try to cut themselves off from this global community. What we're seeing as a reaction to forces people can't control or understand is the rise of nationalism throughout Europe and in other major states around the world. This is the global context we're contending with.

It's the same thing within education. When you're under threat, you tend only to trust those you know and who are like you. Educators have felt under threat for so long now that what we've ended up with as standard practice is a hunkered down community that mistrusts outsiders and alternative voices. Unless you were born in the education space, educators don't trust your credibility or your motives at all. Our default setting is mistrust, and in an environment where you mistrust, your ability to learn, expand, and develop is greatly narrowed.

I think that's exactly what's limiting SEL and Project Based Learning (PBL), a pedagogy that lends itself to SEL.[3] There's loads of money spent trying to break into this community, to get the attention of educators with the latest software program or educational philosophy, but it's like this egg no one can get to because many educators believe that, unless you are one of us, you've got no place in our society. One of the problems that results from this mindset is that, whenever anybody on the inside tries to broaden their perspective and say, "We need to look wider as an education community; we need to embrace and understand more about the world outside the gates; we need to understand more about the world our kids are entering into," they get pushback and resistance. We're in this real conflict right now because educators tend to mistrust an outsider's intentions, even when the outsider is invited by an insider.

Here's a good example of why applying SEL is essential from when I first became the head of Grange Primary School just before September 11, 2001. The school was in the flight path of an airport, so planes were flying low over our school every day on approach and takeoff from an airport just miles away. For sixty years or more, that school had stood in that spot, and kids didn't care or even notice the airplanes. They were blind to it. Kids born in the flight path of an airport just don't see or hear the planes after a while.

A few days after 9/11 I was on the infant playground. A plane came in low to land, and kids dove underneath furniture, benches, and seats. There was panic, and they were crying. These are kids that have never noticed these planes before. But these kids had seen the news; they had seen the images on the television from New York City. They had seen the photos in newspapers, and a few of them had seen them online. Nobody explained it to them because everyone thought they were too young to comprehend. These kids thought the planes were coming to kill them. At that moment, those kids were in no shape to go into a classroom and learn math and do literacy.

We spent a long period of time rebuilding those children's contexts, starting with their emotional reflexes; only then could we create that safe environment in which kids learn best. Every teacher knows that, unless you create an environment where kids feel safe and secure enough to take a risk, fail, make mistakes, and learn, you don't create a learning environment. A learning environment only comes through social-emotional learning.

There is much to learn from making mistakes, even failing. As parents, we often think that the gold standard for our kids is always getting stuff right. As a result, the kid who is a hyper-talented athlete is used to getting stuff right because they're naturally gifted and better than all their peers. They coast their way through school and college, where they do better than others. But then they get to a professional or even semi-professional level where suddenly—for the first time in their lives—they're surrounded by kids who are as talented or more talented than they are. But those kids have never failed. They've never struggled. Therefore, the minute they encounter an obstacle or a barrier and must dip into their bag of emotional skills, they can't find anything valuable; they haven't got any self-esteem or confidence because you only get that when you learn that you can overcome a challenge and overcome failure. You cannot put those tools in your bag when you just get stuff right all the time and never fail. The self-esteem and confidence to pick yourself back up again when you fall only comes from experience. The kids who have had it easy, who have been overpraised and overprotected by their parents, usually end up the ones with the most severe mental health problems as teenagers. On the other hand, the kids who have never had a social-emotional sense of well-being or the support of their parents completely fall by the wayside.

The interesting thing is that the kids that tend to succeed the most are the ones that have had a balance of both. They've had difficult moments in their lives but have been supported in the right way to overcome those problems. That's the sweet spot for which we have to aim our efforts. The really hungry entrepreneurs who end up being our billionaires tend to be the ones who have been through really rocky times in their youths. They failed to get into their college of choice, they come from a broken home, or their first business failed. They failed over and over again until they didn't.

Parents have to ask, "Have I made sure I allow my child to fail?" Our natural biological reflexes are to protect our children, but we are overprotecting them. We are not creating in them the independent abilities, strategies, and emotional security that allow them to fail and to come back from that failure. The biggest lesson for parents is that you have to create an environment where you are supportive of your children but allow them to fail, confident in the knowledge that you've built the emotional environment around them where that child will experience pain and difficulty but will have the confidence to know they can overcome it. If you do that, failure is like weight training. You break down muscle mass for muscle mass to grow back stronger. But if you never do the weights in the first place, muscle mass isn't broken down, which means you can't grow it back stronger.

III. FORECAST FOR THE FUTURE

When I was appointed at Grange Primary School, it was ten years into the school's well-known habitual failure. This school had been failing for ten years, and for ten years people had been flinging "silver bullets" at the problem. A host of government advisors and experts had been going in and briefing the teachers because they thought the only way they were going to keep the school out of closure was to increase academic performance. They would try everything. These advisors would go in and suggest whatever the latest idea was, always emphasizing that it would help with exam results.

When I was appointed, it was evident to me for all kinds of reasons that the school had entirely lost focus on the fact they were dealing with children who were each individual and gloriously organic human beings. They had forgotten about developing people, which is even more relevant in an area of social deprivation than it is in a well-adjusted middle-class community.

Maybe it took courage, or maybe we just had nothing to lose, but we started the entire process all over again. I remember going in and saying, "Stop everything." And I asked one simple, fundamental question that became the foundation for everything that our school was then built on: "What kind of people do we want our kids to be when they leave us?" I wanted to be able to put my hand on my heart and say to the parents, "If you entrust your children to us, these are the kinds of human beings your kids will become."

That became a full stop point to the old way of doing things and sparked a completely different conversation. So how do we ensure that kids have the self-confidence to look people in the eye? How do we ensure kids are articulate enough to explain what they're doing in their classroom, what they're learning, and why that learning is meaningful? If we are going to create kids who have the ability to work in teams and collaborate, all of those behaviors are necessary.

Many kids have dreams, and many kids have fantasies. Until we can solidify them into aspirations, dreams are just fantasies—they're not real. Kids will often say that they want to play in the NFL or they want to be a doctor or they want to be an astronaut. But none of them actually believe it. It's just this kind of fantasy. We turn a dream into an aspiration by building rungs on a ladder that will make that dream tangible. We tell them, "If you want to be an astronaut, you need to be able to do this, and that will lead to this, which could lead to this." Suddenly, that dream moves from fantasy into a potential reality. It's contextualized. Kids can see it. It's de-abstracted and made real. On a social-emotional level, the same is true of life. "Lead a happy life" means nothing to a kid. It's a dream; it's a fantasy. But put rungs on the ladder, and we create something that they can actually grasp onto. The learning connects, and they see the relevance. They see the path and know they can achieve it.

We know that we are doing a good job when we can actually talk to our kids about aspiration and not only do they say, "I want to be a professional soccer player," but they also tell us how they could reasonably and logically give themselves the opportunity to do that without an unrealistic guarantee. Their expectations and plans draw from a wider context. They don't just plan on doing physical education in school, for instance; they don't just plan on studying science. They start seeing how the learning in science and around nutrition can help them become better physical specimens and therefore readier for a professional sports career.

IV. Pathway to Success

We often make the mistake of thinking that all kids come from well-adjusted, safe homes where their families are perpetuating love and security. What we've got to remember is that there are vast waves of children who don't have the good fortune to have that support at home in the U.S., the U.K., and everywhere else around the world. And because of that, social-emotional learning is vital—not only to the sense of well-being and emotional health of our kids, but also to their academic and intellectual achievement now and in the future.

Teachers are like the crew in a casino. And every day your kids are coming into your casino. You're at the roulette wheel, and every time you ask them to engage in learning with you, you're spinning the wheel and rolling the ball. Some of the kids are coming into your classroom with armfuls of poker chips. Some of your kids are walking in with one poker chip.

And here's the challenge. Every time you spin the wheel and roll the ball, the kids with loads of poker chips will throw a few chips on red or black, odd or even. They have the self-esteem and confidence in themselves to engage relentlessly in learning with you. But the kid with one poker chip will show all kinds of behavioral issues, and they'll be clinging to that one poker chip. They don't avoid taking part because they don't want to. Most of the time, they're looking at these games and thinking, "That's a great game. I would love to be able to play that game. But if I put my one poker chip on red and it comes out black, I'm finished." They have thin shields of self-esteem and no confidence in their abilities to learn.

I think the best way to express the importance of social-emotional learning to parents and teachers is to tell them that, if they aren't sure their kids are showing up for formal learning or informal learning with a bag full of self-esteem poker chips, their kids are already in trouble. The only way they build up the poker chips is by gambling and winning and gambling and losing over and over again. It's through those experiences they accumulate the poker chips of self-esteem and confidence.

If you can understand what kind of human traits you want your kids to have when they leave you, you can create a compelling structure to achieve that goal. You'll say, "Okay, if the end game is here, we have to explicitly invest in our kids in this way when they're ten, nine, eight, seven, six, five, four, three." When you have that clarity, you need to create a different form of assessment and a different type of accountability. Teachers can then hold each other accountable as a learning community. You will have the tangible human behaviors in development in your classrooms that form the absolute center-piece of the social-emotional learning that happens in a school community.

It's no accident that those human behaviors become powerful magnets for learning. If you don't have the clarity of those human behaviors at the spine of everything you're doing, then the learning becomes a meaningless game for kids and a playable system for teachers, by which they can guarantee a rise in pay based on performance management metrics. But if you say, "No, the core business of what we're doing is expecting our kids to look like *this* by the time they graduate," everything else then becomes focused on that goal. It gives academics and curriculum a home, a purpose, and a context.

When I was a child at school, we would have a half-hour at the end of the week where we would just talk about current affairs with our teacher. It's one of the things we very deliberately did at Grange Primary School as the last thing on a Friday with all kids, whether they were in the nursery, kindergarten, or whichever grade in school. We would finish the rest of the school week's timetable 45 minutes to an hour early and spend that time with this last session, which we called "Our World This Week."

Kids tend to be very insular. We all tend to be self-centered as children. It's just a natural part of growing up. So we said to the kids, "During the week, look out for stuff in the news, whether it's in a local newspaper, internet, TV news, or just something you've heard your parents discuss. Make a note of it, and on Friday afternoon, we'll sit around as a class and talk through all the issues happening in the world outside of our school that you've noticed during the week." The job of the teacher was to guide students through the discussion, bringing in some of the things they may have been studying in the school that were in relation to the "Our World This Week" discussions.

The reason we did that last every Friday is that, no matter how encouraging it was, our school was still an insular environment. The biggest disconnect between education and life is that education, for most children, is abstracted from their lives. They don't see education as part of their human development or how their lessons fit into the outside world. They see it as very abstract and removed from them, almost to the point where schools for many kids feel like a purgatory that they have to go through before they can live their life. We have to be better at threading the narrative so kids can see how education and formal learning are part of that growth journey. One of the most important things to me about the development of social-emotional learning for our children is that they have to understand how to make sense of their cognitive and emotional development in a broader space than the immediacy of their environment. We have to make sure as educators inside formal or informal settings that we regularly help kids face the world with courage. It is only by doing that and applying their new thinking, development, and emotional and academic responses to a wider world that they process and understand them. We hoped to convey that processing and understanding by ending every school week by consciously bridging the gap between the world and the school for a few minutes.

People often ask, "How are you measuring your success?" They know there are exams, but they also know we aren't using that as our core gauge of how successful we are in our cycle of learning. I say to people that we instead measure the rising aspirations and values of our kids. The individual's value system is an important element. A lot of our kids leave school with no real sense of what value they have as an adult in a local, national, or global community. As all these kids grow and become aware of their talents, strengths, weaknesses, and connections, we want to begin molding in them an understanding of what value they could have as adults in a real society.

We need to assess in kids their growth, talents, abilities, and capacity to operate confidently and effectively in their post-education life. That doesn't happen through a test; it happens through conversation and observation. The ultimate indication for me that we're getting the marriage of holistic and three-dimensional education correct is when children become increasingly informed and can articulate their sense of aspiration, sense of value, and sense of place in the world.

That's how we know we're getting it right.

Editor's Reflection Questions

- When you hear your students' dreams, what steps do you take to help them understand what they can do to turn those dreams into reality?
- With the 24/7 global access today's kids have to the world through television and the internet, have you noticed a change in perspectives and aspirations since you were in school? How can we leverage this global access for the benefit of learners?
- How do you choose to measure SEL in your classroom, both on a day-to-day and long-term basis? What are the indicators that you're getting it right?

NOTES

1. Eleanor Busby, "Schoolchildren should take exams earlier to cope with mental health pressures, says education minister," *The Independent,* February 7, 2018, *https://www.independent.co.uk/news/education/education-news/schoolchildren-exams-more-early-mental-health-pressure-stress-education-nick-gibb-a8199291.html.*

2. For more information about the Programme for International Student Assessment, consult *http://www.oecd.org/pisa/.*

3. For more information about Project Based Learning, consult *https://www.bie.org/.*

Michael Cardona

ADDRESSING STUDENTS' NEED TO SUCCEED IN A DIVERSE DISTRICT

Michael Cardona is Superintendent of Schools for San Marcos Consolidated Independent School District in San Marcos, Texas. Recognized as a turnaround administrator, he helped implement rigorous student performance standards resulting in increased passing rates and higher achievement scores. Lauded by both teachers and administrators for his strong leadership, Cardona has a demonstrated record of strengthening student achievement at all levels.

I. CURRENT STATE OF SEL

Local

For effective social-emotional learning (SEL), the first key is to reduce stress and trauma. As an exercise in reducing stress, the San Marcos Consolidated Independent School District (CISD) in central Texas has adopted "mindfulness, movement, and breathing" as a de-stress mantra.[1] It's not yoga; it's three simple steps to help educators take a moment and stop, capture where they're at, and de-stress, along the lines of "Count to ten."

The next step for effective SEL is to listen to the parents, the kids, and the data and then build the systems around what we learned from listening. We must look at the data; the data will tell us a story, and we can then align our resources with that story. San Marcos CISD was seeing kids coming in with trauma from home. This, of course, affected the teachers dealing with that trauma and caused them stress as well. San Marcos CISD uses a positive behavior intervention system, but our district leadership didn't feel there were enough resources to address the SEL problems we were seeing. It was to the point that we could see the stress on the faces of teachers and students. We established a partnership with Texas State University, and through their School of Social Work, funds were allocated for 15 graduate students to spend their approximately 500 hours per semester of mandatory practicum working as interns with the San Marcos CISD. The partnership has been a win-win for everyone. The interns working with the students and families have shown some great results.

Another example of addressing SEL is when Texas State researchers investigated low Pre-K attendance. According to the data we already had, Pre-K students had the worst attendance in our district. Our initial thought was that parents didn't value Pre-K, but the researchers found something completely different. They found that habits inside the building were contributing to the spread of illness among the children. They were all touching the fountain and the stuffed animals, and they were passing germs back and forth. It's not that parents weren't bringing them; they were just getting sick and staying home. So we set up a cleansing program for that school, and their attendance has since gone up. A full-time parent liaison also works with parents to assist in ensuring that our kids' needs are met.

At the same time, we saw the need for some teacher self-care in our district because if the teachers don't take care of themselves, it just creates an environment that leads to more trauma and stress in the system. We worked with Pure Edge, a nonprofit out of Boston, to provide a program of teacher self-care, and the results have been very promising so far.[2] We've seen some impact with our mid-year assessment, and we're seeing better results in the schools that really focus on taking care of the teachers and the kids.

Regional

The central Texas region has a large percentage of students who come from poverty and require extra resources. San Marcos CISD works regionally with some nonprofit alliances in the Austin area, local business partners, the city of San Marcos, and national businesses to provide support. For instance, all six elementary schools in San Marcos CISD receive support from School Fuel, a nonprofit organization that provides weekly backpack food for about 670 students who we know won't have any food waiting for them when they get home on Friday.[3] This type of relationship addresses trauma due to hunger and malnutrition. The work School Fuel does with the district is invaluable and addresses a major need.

This represents one of several such programs taken advantage of by local schools. San Marcos CISD has an active local community that has really embraced the idea of taking care of the whole child first. A school district can put systems in place to take care of the social-emotional needs of the student and can communicate effectively with the community, which can then support and reinforce the process. San Marcos CISD and our surrounding community are ahead of the curve.

State

With the political climate in Texas at the moment and a large Hispanic population in the San Marcos area, there is a great deal of additional trauma from immigration issues and residency statuses in the local community. While the Constitution is pretty clear about the schools being a safe place, the kids bring with them all the trauma they experience outside of the learning institutions. All our district leadership can do is attempt to insulate students from the outside noise and ensure that the kids are in a safe place to learn.

The powers that be on the state level have to understand that education and social services are not separate. When they don't fund SEL support for the teachers and the kids, they affect essential social services, food stamp programs, and the number of kids locked up in jail. They're all tied together. We all live together, and how one goes, so goes the other.

II. Cost of Maintaining the Status Quo

The San Marcos CISD collects data on the previous year's graduating class after they leave school. There's data to show where kids go to four-year universities, where they go to two-year colleges and trade schools, and how many enter the military. But upon further examination, we noticed that approximately half of all graduated seniors were unaccounted for in the data. After some research, a good portion of the students were found hiding in plain sight; they had never left the area and were working in local businesses and industries in mostly low-paying jobs.

Central Texas is very lucky to be one of the fastest growing regions in the country at the moment, but there are parts of Texas and this country that don't enjoy as robust an economy as we do. There are many parts of the country where jobs are very scarce, and doing nothing to prepare graduating students for the next step in their lives puts an undue strain on the city, region, and workforce. It's a problem when a significant portion of the graduating seniors stay in place locally without bringing advanced degrees and knowledge back to the community and economy.

The business community has been proactive in reaching out to the San Marcos CISD about working together to produce college- and workforce-ready graduates. Groups like the Chamber of Commerce play a crucial role in bridging the school system and the local businesses. They are working with us to develop graduates who think critically and possess the necessary soft skills. The landscape of today's workplace is changing, and education needs to evolve with it. Companies are searching for more social-emotional maturity in an employee than just a few years ago. Google used to hire people based on GPA, but now they hire based on who's going to make the team better in terms of cooperation, collaboration, and creativity.

The papers and local news are full of stories of young people who have made poor choices, and we ask, "Did the parents and the school system fail them with their social-emotional learning? What could we have done differently?" It is our mission as educators to help break the poverty cycle. If there is a family where the first generation of kids enters college and graduates, it changes the entire family for the better forever. San Marcos is a community where the city manager, mayor, and superintendent are all in constant communication about housing patterns because those require specific resources to be provided to the schools those kids are entering. If a battered women's shelter is being built in our district, the principals of the local schools will be alerted so that they can prepare to enroll students who are transient and have experienced a great amount of trauma. Resources and programs will then be allocated and made available to them to help those students.

Poverty causes daily trauma and physically affects the body and nervous system in ways that science is just starting to research. As pediatrician Nadine Burke Harris once said in her TED Talk, "Imagine you're walking in the forest and you see a bear. . . . Your heart starts to pound, your pupils dilate, your airways open up, and you are ready to either fight that bear or run from the bear. And that's wonderful if you're in a forest and there's a bear. But the problem is what happens when the bear comes home every night."[4] When the bear comes home every night, the kids bring that trauma to school with them the next day. How many students have family members who suffer from mental illness? How many have an alcoholic family member? How many have an abusive family member? How many have had a family member commit suicide? The high percentages of divorce and single-parent households, the rising rents in the area that threaten a family's tight budget, the lack of family health insurance and the subsequent rising costs—these all contribute to trauma and stress. These stories need to be understood and told if SEL is going to work.

The San Marcos CISD had a psychologist work with principals around asking students certain questions—getting out of the mindset of judging the kids and instead just listening to what kids are saying or observing kids and knowing what to notice. Students who are always pushing, hitting, or inappropriately touching other kids may be showing signs of trauma. They may or may not be kids who have ADHD, and there is a good chance that they have witnessed that behavior away from the school and have brought the trauma to school with them. The San Marcos CISD School Health Advisory Council is made up of 30 members from all across the community. They are trying to get a solid grasp on social-emotional learning and social-emotional supports for kids that come from high-poverty areas.

Every state has to have a regional service center to help local districts, and local colleges and university systems need to be a critical part of this. It needs to start at the state level, so legislators are strongly encouraged to fund education properly. When they don't fund education correctly or when they don't fund social services to allow them to expand their footprint in the school systems where they're needed, we will continue to have this spinning wheel and go nowhere.

III. Forecast for the Future

Superintendents have to be the champions of SEL and encourage teachers to provide students with the ability to think their way through things in a safe, creative, and therapeutic way. If districts and educators in general don't get a handle on addressing SEL, they will continue to have struggles with the National Alliance for Partnerships in Equity (NAPE), the Program for International Student Assessment (PISA), and other performance measures.[5-6] San Marcos CISD has taken a proactive approach with professional development for teachers and staff around SEL, but talking about SEL and their own stories and the trauma they bring with them causes a lot of teachers to be uncomfortable. Teachers have been programmed to say, "Just give me the curriculum and let me do it," but now we're asking them to figure out the stories of their students and then plan the academics around the students' needs. And that's a very different way of teaching and learning. It's already innovative, but for some, it can be absolutely game-changing. The message we give to the teachers is this: "You know your kids better than we do. You know your content better. But if our district leadership doesn't know what support you need, we can't go to the board to ask for help." San Marcos CISD does have a set of nonnegotiable core commitments: All kids are going to be on or above grade level. All kids are going to be career and college ready. We're going to close achievement gaps. We're going to have a culture of high professionalism and expectations. And we're going to have meaningful and reciprocal community partnerships. Those are the North Star by which we steer. We don't ever tell teachers how to teach a class, but we do tell the teachers and the principals that it is our responsibility to ask them if what they're doing is going to get the kid ready for the real world and what supports they need to achieve that end.

Even with all the support and encouragement, change is difficult for some. Some adults are afraid of change, and those are the people who just need to find another organization. They can't continue doing the same things over and over again and expect different results. If they make mistakes in the best interests of the children, then we can fix those mistakes. If they just do the same things that haven't worked, then we're going to be spinning our wheels for a long time. And when they do that, the students know they're not genuine and authentic, and that's when we've lost the students. Trying to get the students' trust back and convincing them that adults honestly mean well is time-consuming, exhausting, and occasionally futile.

IV. Pathway to Success

Universities and state and national organizations need to update the way they train superintendents so they can become the champions of SEL. The E3 Alliance—an education collaborative based in Austin, Texas, which closely collaborates with partner school districts, including San Marcos CISD—is very good at what they do.[7] They look at the whole child—attendance, truancy, schedules, and social-emotional supports. But conferences currently touting SEL become nothing more than networking opportunities rather than learning meetings. Our regional service centers in Texas need to be more focused so that superintendent meetings with twenty other superintendents are not just about politics. The meetings need to be about who has a good model to make a difference and change outcomes for our kids, not about how bad our legislators are. That positive dialogue is what we lack right now state-wide in Texas.

The collaboration that comes as a natural and intricate part of SEL teaches kids how to get along with kids who don't look like them. Our district leadership firmly believes in socioeconomically diverse classrooms and thinks that simply being involved in a diverse classroom learning environment is going to make for a much better graduate in the end. When kids are with other kids who don't look like them and have different thoughts, they hear different viewpoints. The curriculum has to be structured in a way that encourages debate and dialogue and inspires class and individual projects based on solving problems in the local community.

We also have to be very intentional about teaching diversity. We do that by exposing children to field trips designed so that they start seeing people who don't look like them being successful. Even though San Marcos is home to Texas State University and the University of Texas is just a few miles up the road in Austin, there are kids who have never set foot on a university campus. Both campuses are very diverse, so San Marcos CISD has been purposeful in putting our K–12 kids in that setting so that they see kids who don't look like them and kids who do look like them working side-by-side and being successful.

As we find out more about the effects of poverty on the brain, how the brain works around SEL, and the successes of those systems that have good SEL supports, more educators and districts will pick up on it. The information has been around for a while, but SEL is like a circle on a Venn diagram that's starting to intersect with the circles for curriculum and teachers to create the student outcomes that we all want and desire.

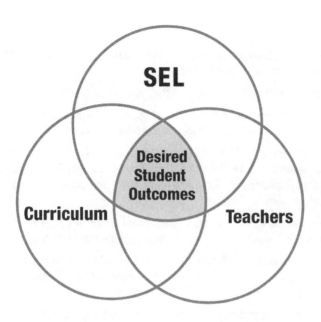

Editor's Reflection Questions

- In what ways is the district described in this chapter similar to or different from your district or community? Which strategies used by this district would you like to borrow? Which might you adjust?
- Have you previously thought about diversity as a topic that needs to be taught? What are the specific needs your learners have in this area, and how can you teach it better?
- Would you describe your school or classroom as trauma-informed or trauma-sensitive? If not, how can you improve to meet the needs of the many students suffering trauma?

NOTES

1. To learn more about the San Marcos Consolidated Independent School District, visit our website *www.smcisd.net.*

2. To learn more about Pure Edge, visit their website *pureedgeinc.org/.*

3. To learn more about School Fuel and the support they provide to children in San Marcos, visit their website *https://www.schoolfuelsanmarcos.org/.*

4. Nadine Burke Harris. "How childhood trauma affects health across a lifetime." Filmed September 2014. TED video, 15:59. Posted February 2015. *https://www .ted.com/talks/nadine_burke_harris_how_childhood_trauma_affects_health _across_a_lifetime.*

5. To learn more about the National Alliance for Partners in Equity and the perfomance measures they use, visit their website *https://www.napequity.org/.*

6. To learn more about the Program for International Student Assessment and the performance measures they use, visit their website *https://nces.ed.gov /surveys/pisa/.*

7. To learn more about the E3 Alliance and their work in Central Texas, visit their website *http://e3alliance.org/.*

Kyla Krengel

IMPLEMENTING DISTRICT-WIDE SEL WITH INTENTIONALITY

Kyla Krengel currently serves as the Director of Social and Emotional Learning with Metro Nashville Public Schools. She has worked to bring SEL supports to administrators, teachers, and students through her work in the district as a classroom teacher, trainer, and assistant principal. Kyla also serves as co-chair of the Alignment Nashville Behavioral Health Committee, which will be hosting the Music City SEL Conference in the summer of 2018.

I. CURRENT STATE OF SEL

Local

In Metro Nashville Public Schools (MNPS), social-emotional learning (SEL) is stronger now than it has ever been.[1] The administration of MNPS has spent six solid years intentionally integrating SEL into the culture. Over that time, we have collected good data that has allowed us to identify some strengths that we have as a district, some areas of concern, and some resources that are available to support schools.

MNPS recently switched to the Multi-Tiered System of Supports (MTSS) to help make sure the conversations about SEL at the district level and in individual schools focus on the whole child.[2] For instance, because of behavioral issues shown by the data in Tier 1 schools that were just starting their journey, we decided to focus those schools on building their SEL practices as quickly as possible. One of the very first things addressed was building capacity—they must have capacity to make sure that the work is being done and being done well. We also have to realize and accept on all levels that this isn't one-time training. This is ongoing work that never ends. We created a walk-through rubric so that everyone knows exactly what we're looking for when our team walks into a school. MNPS worked with our research and assessment department as well as the Collaborative for Academic, Social, and Emotional Learning (CASEL) to create the walkthrough rubric.[3]

SAMPLE COMPONENTS OF MNPS SEL WALKTHROUGH RUBRIC

Schoolwide Environment	Classroom Instruction	Classroom Environment
Atmosphere in Common Areas	Expectations and Learning Objectives	Classroom Atmosphere
Student Work Displayed	Explicit Teaching of SEL Skills	Student Behavior
Student Relationships	Teacher Feedback and Monitoring	Student Voice
Adult Relationships	Student Engagement	Classroom Procedures

Adapted from the official MNPS SEL Walkthrough Rubric, provided courtesy of Metro Nashville Public Schools

The rubric looks at three big areas. The first is the overall schoolwide environment. Are students being welcomed? What are the relationships between the adults? What are the relationships between the students and then the students and adults? What is the vision and the mission of the school? Within their vision and mission, are they looking at the whole child and making sure that they're meeting the needs of the entire child?

The second area we look at is how SEL is being integrated into the academics and the classroom. What are the teachers' standards, objectives, and expectations? Are they strictly academic, or are they expressing that they're going to be looking at SEL throughout the lesson as well as academics? Are students collaborating? Are they reflecting throughout the lesson? Is there interactive pedagogy that is engaging for students? We also look at engagement versus compliance. Are the students paying attention and participating because that's what they're supposed to do, or are they truly engaged in the lesson? And is SEL explicitly taught within the classroom?

The third area we look at is classroom management and environment. Are there rules? Are there procedures so that the students are set up for success in the classroom? If there's a problem, how are the students behaving? How does the teacher handle a problem within the classroom? Do the students have a voice in the classroom?

The district and the region as a whole are learning to speak the same language. Knowledge is being shared as a community, and cultural foundations are being built. Knowing that this is an individual process and journey, every school is in a different place with SEL and their approach. Some schools are just beginning this journey. They've chosen their Tier 1 approach this year, and they're having their administrative teams go through training. Other schools are a little further along and have already begun the process of integrating SEL into academics. Some schools have already had SEL leadership teams on campus for a few years and have changed discipline practices from a punitive to a much more restorative philosophy.

MNPS is seeing progress with our SEL, whereas, for other districts, the SEL director is a new position in charge of a department that they're still creating. They're trying to figure out how they want to create a rollout plan around this work.

State

Budgets are tight. Almost every district is facing budget cuts nationwide, and Tennessee is no different. Our policy experts and lawmakers need to understand what social-emotional learning is and how critical it is to the future. Getting that point across is something that school districts and administrations struggle with across the country. Some legislators don't truly understand what this is, so they hesitate to support it. They say, "Teachers already do this, and those things are the responsibility of the parents and already happen at home."

Legislators need to know and understand that students are coming to school with trauma from outside the building, and as children, they don't have the skills, strategies, and experience to cope with it. They need to understand that teachers are asking and begging for more support around social-emotional learning work because teachers are the ones who deal with the students and their trauma every school day. According to the district's data, around 43% of the students themselves are saying that they're not engaged at school. The students are also saying that they want to be heard and to have more time with their teachers one-on-one, talking and building relationships. Students want to feel valued outside of the classroom. They don't want to feel like just a number.

II. Cost of Maintaining the Status Quo

The district and administration have to create an environment where every single person within a school—every child and every adult, including parents, bus drivers, custodians, front office staff, and so on—feels they are a part of that community and that they belong there with a connection to each other. It's those relationships that are missing in so many lives in today's world. Expelled students who suffer punitive discipline are cut off from any help or assistance the school can offer through restorative discipline. They are set adrift in a world they are ill-prepared to navigate.

One of the main areas the district, region, and state look at is the data gathered on discipline. What's the percentage of student suspension? Who's being suspended? For what? Where do these students end up in five years? Ten years? We look at attendance data. If students don't want to come to school, then why? What's the concern at home? What services are available to help these students and these families? The district and state also look at the regional mental health numbers and factors. How many students are being recommended for extra support? Are their needs being met within the school and within the classroom? Districts and administrations are always requesting more resources, more people to come out and support, and more money to make the programs work. But as much as we want to make this dream come true, with current budgets and future trends, there is not enough support or resources from the states for this work to happen right now.

A great deal of the SEL work that MNPS does is centered around the relationships between the students, between the teachers and students, and between individuals and the community. The questions that the district and the administration ask are designed to create an environment that welcomes the whole child and gives them a safe and inclusive education community. The conversations that the district and schools have are so important: Do the students feel connected to somebody? Do they have somebody to talk to? Do they have somebody that is looking out for them? Every student should feel that they belong in school, and every student should feel significant. They need to feel that they belong because, if they don't, they're going to find that sense of belonging elsewhere.

Parents, teachers, administrators, legislators, and even students get caught up in a score or a grade, and everyone forgets that in the end they're dealing with very young humans trying to figure it all out. It is an SEL skill, not an academic skill, to teach students that they can be successful in school, in relationships, and in life. We need to give them a safe place where they can come and have these conversations and figure some things out. SEL is about building those relationships and then providing that safe environment where our students are able to have the important conversations. If we don't help them learn how to be valuable and useful members of the community, who will? Without restorative discipline to teach them how to take responsibility for their words and deeds and make amends to live peacefully in a community, students will continue to feel excluded and shunned by punitive discipline. They will continue to react as outsiders and exiles toward their educational institutions and communities, with occasional tragic results.

III. Forecast for the Future

In Metro Nashville Public Schools, we feel that we are ahead of the curve with our SEL program and implementation. We are continually expanding and growing our efforts through professional development meant to bring the latest research on social-emotional learning into the academics of the everyday classroom.

MNPS has an online page—available to anyone—where we keep all of our resources and lesson plans gathered by the education community. There are resources that teachers can use centered around interactive learning structures. If they want to make their lesson more engaging, the district will share some ideas on how to do that as well.

The schools and teachers also do a lot of modeling with the students. The teachers are supported and given training, a lot of examples, and many tools that they can take into their classroom and use. They always know that they have mentors and other teachers available to help support them. The network is always growing in the district and in the schools as more experienced instructors share their expertise, ideas, and wisdom.

The district anticipates that the results will continue in the right direction and that the satisfaction of students, staff, parents, and the community at large will continue to grow as SEL becomes a standard part of MNPS's academic tradition, educational curriculum, and community culture.

IV. Pathway to Success

To make SEL an intricate part of the culture on an organic level, there needs to be an understanding and agreement by all parties involved on what social-emotional learning really is. This definition has to be an understanding shared by everyone, from the central district office down to the individual schools, teachers, and parents.

We need the commitment from the school as well as the central office that SEL is a priority. It means having the capacity and the will to keep working with schools continuously, supporting them, and coaching them. We have to have people, we have to have money, and we have to have time to do all of that. The conversations with legislators and lawmakers now can't be focused on just academics; we need to be looking at social-emotional learning as well as academics. They need to understand that this is a long-term process. There won't be stunning results in weeks or months.

The administration needs to keep helping teachers understand how to build relationships with their students. Essentially, we've got to know our kids in order to be able to help them grow.

Districts and schools need to be aware of their core competencies and capacity for living them out. They need to ensure that they keep their professional development current and updated. Even the best teachers can't teach something they don't know about with something they don't have. We must develop practical skills and establish communication strategies that build confidence and competence for both the student and the teacher in the classroom, in order to ensure continued academic and social-emotional growth and success.

Parents need to find out what their school's Tier 1 approach is—restorative practices, Professional Development Information System, or SEL foundation—because there is a different language for each one of them. It's helpful if the families are aware of the administration's approach to social-emotional learning. For obvious reasons, they need to have a consistent language at home as well as in school. For instance, if their school is focused on the SEL foundation, then at home they would talk about core competency or what "I Can" statement the student is working on in math class. It's about maintaining that consistent language and message around the whole child as they continue to learn and grow throughout their entire day.

Editor's Reflection Questions

- Think about your school or the schools in your district. How would you evaluate them according to the excerpt of the MNPS SEL Walk-through Rubric on page 104?
- Does your district have an explicit definition of what SEL means in your schools? If so, how does this facilitate effective implementation? If not, how does this create challenges?
- What is one SEL practice you wish were implemented in your school or district, and how can you advocate for it to happen?

NOTES

1. To learn more about Metro Nashville Public Schools and its efforts to promote social-emotional learning, visit *https://www.mnps.org/*.

2. To learn more about the creation and structure of the Multi-Tiered System of Supports, visit *https://sites.ed.gov/osers/tag/multi-tiered-system-of-supports/*.

3. To learn more about the Collaborative for Academic, Social, and Emotional Learning, better known as CASEL, visit *https://casel.org/*.

Rebecca Townsend

STRENGTHENING CONNECTIONS TO IMPROVE MENTAL HEALTH

Rebecca Townsend is a senior licensed psychological examiner and a licensed professional counselor. She has worked in the field of mental health for 20 years and has extensive experience working with military service members and their families. She was in the first class of graduates to receive a post-master's certificate in military and veteran behavioral health through the Department of Defense's Center for Deployment Psychology, and she has completed professional trainings in stepfamily development, couples communication, and parenting.

I. Current State of SEL

As a licensed professional counselor and mental health provider working in private practice near Fort Campbell, one of the largest army divisions, I consider the home to be the primary classroom for social-emotional learning (SEL). Parents and all other primary caregivers of students are often the most important teachers of social-emotional learning. When parents are not at their emotional best, it has a direct impact on their children. By the time I see children in my office, they're typically already in a deficit of social-emotional learning skills.

Since 2010, I've seen a general increase in the number of children coming into my practice, with a significant increase in the number of young children. The soldiers in our military community are deployed very rapidly. They deploy, come home months later, undergo several months of very intensive training, and then deploy again. The rapid and constant deployments have slowed down a bit, but the residual effect of this cycle has unfortunately caught up to the families and dependents of many of these soldiers. I'm also beginning to see the effect on many children of the combat veterans who are no longer in active service to our nation but still live in our community.

Overall, I would say we have a big challenge on our hands. One of the things I do in my practice is make sure I see the parents first before I see their child. I always want to look at what is going on with the parents so I can use that experience to make a template through which to view the child and the child's behaviors. It is undeniable that a child's social-emotional state has a great deal to do with the parents and their behaviors.

Mental Health in Military Communities

Anxiety is something I have seen more of in recent years. With this increase has also come more severe characteristics that would meet the diagnostic criteria for generalized anxiety disorder. I don't specifically diagnose that right off the bat because I think a lot of it is temporary and an adjustment to changes being made in the home. The anxiety in my community is usually aligned with one of the parents being deployed. There has been an increase of brigades deployed from Fort Campbell in 2018. An Army brigade is approximately 3,000–4,000 soldiers, so if we have a full brigade deployment, I'll inevitably see a sharp increase in parents seeking mental health assistance for their kids. The most common symptom the parents cite is "anxiety."

With all kinds of people from all walks of life—adults, children, couples, or families, both in the field and in my office—anxiety appears contagious. It is something that moves from one person experiencing anxiety into another person who is close to them. Since children are susceptible to what surrounds them, it doesn't surprise me when a parent who wants to bring their child in discloses during the pre-interview that they too are experiencing some form of anxiety. The anxiety has a way of carrying over to the child. As a general rule, kids are going to handle whatever mental health challenges they're encountering in the same fashion as their parents are handling them.

Social-emotional learning has to be done in the community because we can't expect real change if we just teach a kid the skill sets in school and then have them go home, where they don't have that shared experience with their parents. For real change to stick, social-emotional learning has to be a community-wide connection. To establish an effective community-wide connection, there must be more opportunities for parents to be involved at the ball game or on the soccer field. As a society, we are consumed with those types of activities, so let's drill some SEL into children and families in these settings. It's collaborating during these social events that helps us become a more cohesive community. If we can share meals, that's all the better. Years ago, there were lots of barbecues and weekend family gatherings in the military community. These seem to have faded with the deployment cycle.

Remember, we're going on 17 years of war now. The military folks are tired. At about the end of the previous decade, families became more tired and stressed out and began to isolate more frequently. The informal family support system that the military had in place for many generations broke down. They are exhausted, and they're barely keeping their own families in place. For many of them, the idea of moving into a larger community with bigger connections now that they're out of active service can appear too exhausting.

One of the important things to maintain in the military community is the conversation around emotions and emotional health. It is important that it's not considered a taboo subject and that we realize and accept our emotional health is as important as our physical health. The emotions we allow to cycle in our brains are just as important as what we put into our bodies.

A common fallacy in the military community is that someone who displays emotions cannot serve in the military effectively. That's what they are taught in the training for military personnel: they cannot be emotional. That can be a life-or-death issue in a combat zone, but it's challenging for a military parent to turn on the emotions again once they get home to their families.

Many service members also experience moral injury from war, and that seeps out into their families as well. There's a pervasive fear among military families that, if they show up in a new community with their "broken" family, they're going to be "found out" and seen as the military family who can't hold it together. They fear that the situation will have an impact on their spouse's career and that their children will not be accepted in their new school and community.

Fear keeps us sick. Isolation keeps us sick. We're not going to solve any problem alone. It truly does take a village, but we have to know that the village is safe and that it's not going to come back and bite us for being vulnerable. In the military, mental health problems often have a way of being perceived as weakness. Parents will insist that their children are not experiencing any emotional health problems and that no mental health problems exist in their family. They end up running through medical doctors trying to find out what's going on with their kids because anxiety can show up as poor sleep cycles, both lack of sleep and too much sleep. Anxiety can be somatic responses such as headaches, stomachaches, and other general symptoms. Their children will often also begin to rely on coping mechanisms. As adults, we all have our own "medications," both healthy and unhealthy; children simply have their own ways of coping, both healthy and unhealthy, as well. They will isolate themselves or do what I call "numbing out," which can include behaviors like overusing video games or overeating.

These all combine to become an indescribable illness in the children, and medical doctors are not able to properly treat it. Once any medical condition has been ruled out, then we can look at the children and their families and ask, "Okay, what's going on with them emotionally?" It's important for all providers to take account of the system and factor in those emotional variables. We cannot just treat one piece of the issue, send children back to their lives, and expect all of it to be better. There are still other pieces that must be addressed for healing to occur. A family is like a baby mobile that hangs over a crib. If one piece starts acting erratically, all the other pieces move too.

You can't take one piece out and put it back in because the other pieces are still moving. We've got to work with the whole system.

In my community, we have a huge shortage of mental health providers. We need the insurance companies to step up to the plate and provide quality care because our communities depend on it more and more. If mental health availability increases and the stigma of admitting to a problem decreases, people will be able to go and seek help. They can get what they need without feeling discouraged, isolated, or disconnected.

It is also my experience as a mental health provider that we heal best in community. When we're in a therapeutic group setting, the majority of our own healing is done by observing someone else's work to get healthy and hearing their story about their struggles and successes. By hearing someone else's story, we know we're not alone or isolated, and it gives us hope. We know that someone has shared our experience and come out on top in the end. Our task as counselors is to provide a safe space for these conversations to happen. One thing we are missing out on right now is being able to have shared experiences and hear each other's journeys and stories to share empathy with each other. It's essential to let the parents, as well as the kids, know they're not alone in what they're experiencing and handling.

We need to see more safe spaces created for therapeutic groups in our school system. And we don't just need a physical space—we also need a space on the school schedule so that SEL can become a priority and more of these important conversations can take place. An elementary school recently invited me to do a six-week parenting class. The school's parent cohort is about 60% active duty military, and that percentage doesn't include the high number of veterans who settled in the area after their discharges. The class gave the parents a great safe space to have an amazing "aha" moment together. There were a lot of people saying, "Oh, my gosh, we're not alone!" Their neighbors were struggling with this very same thing, but they were afraid to say it out loud.

II. Cost of Maintaining the Status Quo

If we continue to move forward as we are currently moving and don't create environments based on social-emotional learning, we are headed toward communities of isolation. Being in isolation causes depression and anxiety; it causes a fight-or-flight response. Those are things that I have seen personally, both in clients and in people whom I've walked beside on this journey of life. I have seen that darkness manifest itself in their lives when they maintain a state of isolation.

We cannot survive in isolation. That's not how we exist as a species. As a mental health provider, I admit that, initially, isolation is comfortable and feels safe. But unless we consciously push ourselves and get into an uncomfortable spot to intentionally challenge our isolation, it's where we'll continue to be, and we can't live that way forever. It's good to be uncomfortable at times. That's when growth happens. Staying where we are out of fear, there's deadness in that. We all have seen this in families at restaurants isolated because of their devices. There's no interaction, no commonality, no saying, "How was your day? I had a rough day, and here's how I've dealt with it." Parents have been passing on their wisdom to their kids for millennia by telling stories around the fire or dinner table, but we're not sharing those experiences anymore. That's a problem.

I'm a stepmom, and I monitor our 14-year-old's cell phone. Flipping through his text messages recently, I saw something that seemed mean and nasty—something kids call "roasting." I called him on it; I said, "Hey, buddy, this is a little harsh. What's going on with this?" He explained "roasting" to me, and when he did, it hit me that we had never taught him how to text. We'd never shown him our cell phones and said, "This is an appropriate text."

When I was growing up, I heard my parents on the phone all the time, and I knew what constituted an appropriate conversation. I knew how to answer my phone and ask for someone politely. But we're not teaching kids that today. We keep our cell phones strictly private, and that's a danger. We're missing out on opportunities to continue to teach our children how to treat one another and how to engage in conversation with each other properly on these devices. If we continue what we're doing and keep going down this path, we're just going to end up isolated and depressed, lacking the skills to engage appropriately and meaningfully with one another.

In my experience, parents are afraid to go against what they perceive to be the norm. It's like social overprotection. They don't want their children being made fun of because they don't have a cell phone or can't play a particular video game. They initially think they are making life easier for their kids, but in reality, they're making it so much harder for their children in the long run by delivering everything they demand. We often project our own pain and our own experience onto those we're raising, and we desperately try to spare them the same harsh lessons we had to learn. We remember our discomfort and say, "I don't want my child to be made fun of because it was so painful when I experienced that." But the truth is we survived. We made it, and we also learned a lot from those painful experiences.

We have to resist that impulse to help our kids be "cool." Instead, we have to go out into an uncomfortable space and trust our intuition that's telling us to go against what we see as the current norm. It's hard. It's really hard. But it's necessary. We have to challenge ourselves and be uncomfortable as adults. We must speak to our kids. We have to speak our truth and say, "This is hard for me. I want to be like so-and-so's mom who got her kid the 'thing.' And I know you want to be like that kid too. But here's our value system. Here's what our long-term goal is." That's stepping things forward and advancing the social-emotional component. That's giving them a skill set, a set of tools for them to use. That's what I try to teach parents to do. I tell them not just to lay down the law but to explain the long-term effects of that law as well. It's important to let your kids know why you are choosing to do A rather than B.

We also need to give our kids more credit cognitively and intellectually. If we say, "Because I said so," we're not being human with them. We're not sharing our experience of life and the wisdom we've gathered. There has to be a shoulder-to-shoulder experience with kids. They know what they hear and what they see. If we give them the dots, they will connect them.

The age-old hierarchy you enforce by saying, "I'm in charge, and that's why," has its time and place, but for a family's long-term well-being, you need to learn to say, "Life is tough, and we're always making hard decisions. It's hard for me to guide you in this new way, but I'm going to be right here beside you. This is new for both of us." When I'm working with families, that's the conversation I coach them to have.

III. FORECAST FOR THE FUTURE

One of the things that we see pop up the most when we talk about the social-emotional competencies with our military families is the issue of self-management. We have combat veterans who struggle with that management once they're outside of the military structure. They are set adrift without the daily support they received in their units through their camaraderie with fellow soldiers. My hope for our military population is that we will continue to reduce the stigma against seeking mental health assistance. We need to teach them empathy and compassion. We need to show them how to have conversations about their emotions by first teaching them how to self-manage them in a safe space without shame or fear. As we do that, the effect will trickle down to their families and children. Once they become more comfortable seeking mental health help in the outside world and learning new ways to manage their own emotions, then the children are going to learn by example.

Our job is to try to help them once again respond in healthy emotional ways within their family unit. It is crucial that families have some definite ways to do that, some good, solid programs and procedures in place. Even if that's something as simple as sitting with each other or playing games together, the important part is being in connection with them. As a way to bridge the gap, I often tell families, "You need to laugh together. Be silly together. Sing together. Rake up a pile of leaves and jump in them together. Be in connection with each other."

Especially for military family members, that's how we're going to start to stir these emotions again. They're not going to excite emotions by being in isolation. It only happens when they're in connection with their kids and their spouse, enjoying emotional experiences together. When I talk about emotions, many people in the military population get scared. They say, "I don't want to cry with my family." So I often say, "It's easier to start out with the fun emotions, so do that first. Let's make sure you all have fun together." But they also need to understand that crying is just one of the numerous ways we experience emotions.

We also need to remember to get on our kids' levels. I mean that literally—I sit on the floor of my office with kids. I don't have them sit on a chair and look at me; I put together blocks and puzzles on the floor with them. I have to get out of my comfort zone to connect with them, but it is always completely worth it. As we play together, it's helping both of us. By playing with a child, you do two things at once: you give yourself a healthy outlet to tackle your own anxiety, and you help reduce the anxiety of the child by giving them a fun experience with a less anxious adult.

IV. Pathway to Success

My hope for our future is that we return to meeting in person instead of just online. We need more human contact and more diverse social gatherings. We need more face-to-face events with fewer screens and more connectedness. We need to share our laughter and our joy. We need to allow wonderful community interaction to become our thrill instead of playing video games that isolate by their very nature. If we can follow this path, we're going to have more eyeball-to-eyeball, heart-to-heart connection in our communities.

And it's important to prioritize creating these connections alongside our kids. I know it's hard to be vulnerable in spaces where we're not used to being vulnerable and where the risk is high. It's hard to take that leap of faith and be vulnerable. But we're not talking about going to an obedience class with our dog—we're talking about the futures of our precious children. We're not just raising kids; we're raising future adults. The outcome we want is for the kids we are raising to be adults who can live in their own truth. We want them to be adults who can listen to another person's truth and accept it even if they don't agree with it. It's that diversity that creates such a rich community of meaningful connections. The diversity fertilizes our growth as individuals and as a community. Is that idealistic? Yes, absolutely! But why not be idealistic? We know that what we're doing now is obviously not working. We keep seeing the effects of living with high anxiety and isolation, and we see that it's not a healthy place for us to be. Living in that state of isolation reinforces itself because the isolation reinforces our fears.

We need to take a baby step into a place of vulnerability and see if we can create a little more trust in one another. I'm not saying we're going to jump off the cliff and immediately fix everything. We can't go from complete isolation to complete connectedness in one giant step. There are steps in between. But when we take a step and learn to feel comfortable there, we will experience a little bit of relief from our anxiety and isolation, and that relief will give us the hope and encouragement to keep stepping toward one another. We will be ready to take the next step, and at some point, we'll look back and say, "Wow, that was worth it, and it really wasn't so hard." Then we can encourage the next group behind us to do the same thing.

Editor's Reflection Questions

- Do your students have access to mental health professionals in the school or through community partnerships? If so, how have you leveraged these professionals to address students' needs? If not, how can you advocate to get your students access?
- How can schools become a place where students and families know their stresses and anxieties are understood and supported?
- Was there a time when a student was suffering from trauma or another mental health issue that felt beyond your ability to address? What action did you take to ensure the student got help?

Kathy Wade

GAINING WHOLE-COMMUNITY BUY-IN FOR SEL

Kathy Wade is co-founder and CEO of Learning Through Art, a 501(c)(3) whose mission is to provide quality performing arts programs in support of arts integrated education, literacy, community development and engagement, and multicultural awareness and understanding. The recipient of numerous civic, social, and artistic awards, Kathy has spent more than 25 years building community in the Cincinnati metropolitan area and beyond.

I. CURRENT STATE OF SEL

My experiences have shaped the simple approach I take to understanding and implementing social-emotional learning (SEL). It's very basic. It has nothing to do with levels of understanding. It requires a simple approach to effectively disseminate the lesson and the wisdom you are sharing. Simple acts are the ones that people hold onto, grow from, and keep teaching. We're always trying to share the simple acts because that's where the growth lies.

When I first started practicing SEL, I didn't realize it had a name. It wasn't really a "thing" yet, but it just seemed to be best practice. It's important to account for kids' social-emotional needs, so that's what we did. But now it has become much more of a movement nationwide. SEL is now understood to be an important part of formal education. This doesn't detract from the efforts of those who were doing SEL before it was known as SEL, but rather makes the current efforts much stronger by providing the shared language to guide well-planned SEL practices.

A successful social-emotional framework is a community in action, and we're seeing a lot more understanding of this concept. Making SEL sustainable requires engaging with the broader community beyond the school walls, including family and community members. It means understanding their needs and challenges and making everyone a part of the effort. Schools continue to broaden their understanding of this while developing their own programs and engaging strategic partners to make more intentional SEL efforts.

SEL can come in a lot of different forms and fashions, but the language you use to dispense that information and frame experiences for a child is the key driver. It's important to use a common language so that both child and parent can be engaged and on the same page. With a community event, we keep in mind the concept that it's for "kids of all ages," whether they're elementary school students or 99-year-olds. Anyone who participates can become hooked on the programming because we use a simple common language. I've seen how all members of the community can rally around SEL when they are included, communicated with, and accounted for.

Local

My hometown is Cincinnati, Ohio, and like most cities, Cincinnati can be seen as a microcosm of our global community. We have one school in our city with 89 different languages being spoken, which provides quite an illustration of how many different cultures are represented locally. We also see this in programs that bring together members of the community whose lives may not meaningfully intersect without a concerted effort. When kids and families have the opportunity to participate in events where the only agenda is to meet their neighbors, their social needs are met in a powerful way. When this is taken a step further, there is the opportunity to gain an expanded understanding of what it means to be a neighbor; people learn that neighbors aren't just those in our schools, on our streets, or even in our cities and states. Instead, we realize that all people on the planet are our neighbors. It may sound like an enormous undertaking to bring kids and families to such a broad understanding of the term, but I've witnessed firsthand how quickly the idea catches on when we start by introducing them to peers across the community. We must keep it simple. We tell people, "While you're here, we need you to turn to each other and meet your neighbor."

Facilitating opportunities for kids to broaden their horizons and meet new neighbors helps them take an immense step forward in their social-emotional development and their growth as citizens, and it can all be done without having to force the lesson. At our multicultural community events, we say, "Today we want you to make sure that you meet somebody that has one thing different from you, whether it's eye color, hair color, shoe size, hand size, or foot size. You may meet a purple person, chartreuse person, or a green person. If one thing is different from you, introduce yourself." Kids want to meet people who are different.

Creating a sense of community begins with being welcoming and inviting. I believe in the commitment to having open doors. People can choose to walk through the door or not, but my job is to provide the invitation and the opportunity. We know the arts are supportive of SEL by their very nature, so I say, "I want you to come over and meet all the people in our community. Come and hear what kind of music other people like. We're going to have the music that you enjoy as well so that they can hear your type of music." These are messages that bridge divides. We can all learn what others like but also know that they will learn about what we like. More often than not, people will choose to walk through that kind of open door. Understanding, accepting, and embracing our differences is a major component of SEL.

None of this is meant to indicate that we, as a society, have arrived at a place where everyone is naturally aware of the richness of the multicultural landscape around them. When we host an event, we're doing that to draw upon the fact that there are more similarities than not within our community. Far too often there's a tendency not to discuss that. People seem to want to categorize themselves as individuals and differentiate themselves from large swaths of society rather than talk about inclusion and belonging. Even within the borders of our city, we have neighbors with backgrounds, interests, and talents beyond what most residents have experienced. With as multicultural, multilingual, and multi-everything as we are, our cultural mosaic continues to be underestimated. The idea that it's simply about black and white stubbornly persists, but we are far beyond that now.

The Broader Community

To gain real traction, SEL programs need to be widely effective. Within schools and other educational settings, there are important discussions taking place. Educators believe in the importance of SEL but understandably won't commit to a program unless it really works. Teachers lack spare time, so implementation needs to be practical as well. These are important considerations that can be satisfied by looking at the evidence of what happens in our communities.

In order to make SEL effective and practical, there's a need to identify the common bond between the child we're working with and their context. Their environment shapes the way they interact with the local school and larger community. When thinking about the best ways to integrate social-emotional learning into content, we must remember that SEL is an experience. There's a visceral component to it that we may not feel comfortable with as adults. Grown-ups often like to categorize information, but when we're busy classifying community activism, we end up staying in the office and missing what is going on at the ground level with young people.

Not long ago, I had the opportunity to give a presentation at a statewide symposium meeting with early childhood educators. I spoke about the connection between arts and adverse childhood experiences (ACEs). I asked, "How can arts programs help to address the challenges of childhood trauma?" When we were having a group discussion near the end, the focus turned to how to publicize the work we're all doing. How do we talk about ACEs? How do we talk about SEL? How do we speak with people who need this information? Essentially, how do we communicate?

At the beginning of the day, we had all gone around and introduced ourselves and our work. I must admit that sitting there and listening to everyone tell who they were and what they have done felt a bit intimidating. I'm no slouch, and it still felt a little overwhelming. Yet when we got to the time where we had to talk about action, I realized we're all facing the same challenges. No matter what our role or affiliation, we all have to work together to make it happen.

To push things forward, we must be cognizant of what's happening in the classroom. What do we see, and what is missing? If we look closely, we can identify the gaps to fill in, and maybe then we will develop plans to fill them. As educators and others in decision-making positions, we're often hearing the same voices and thinking the same way. If we're all thinking the same and remaining stumped on how to begin, we're not making progress. None of this is helping the kids.

What is the first thing we must understand? We must refocus the lens from the clinical, the theoretical, the clipboard research—this practice or that syndrome and so forth. We must expand the view because, in the end, clinical thinking is not what will spur action or engagement. Programs for SEL will gain buy-in at all levels, from administrator to teacher to student, if they allow an interactive process where everyone can see the real benefits and results.

II. Cost of Maintaining the Status Quo

When I started working with kids on literacy programs that had a foundation in addressing their social-emotional needs, we found that kids really respond. Taking care of kids' basic needs for emotional support, safety, mental health, and belonging makes them more engaged and more prepared to learn, period. However, an intuitive approach to SEL without specifically calling it out as a focus can only take you so far. Without an intentional plan it becomes difficult to continue focusing on SEL, and it certainly becomes a challenge, if not impossible, to improve the way we do SEL without that focus. To reach the next level and sustain success, it needs to be better understood and prioritized by all parties.

We run the risk of losing SEL and other elements of a well-rounded education if they are not part of the education law or accountability requirements. If schools think strategically, they can make it happen. As an example, we started two decades ago by simply trying to figure out how to get kids to read who didn't want to read. To do this, our solution was to develop an arts integration program. However, No Child Left Behind was in place at the time, and its focus on standardized testing, combined with budget cuts in many districts, meant that arts education was being pulled out of schools.[1] Everyone who was teaching the arts had to figure out, as an artist and an educator, how to align their curriculum and program to what was going on in the school's or district's overall curriculum. We had to make sure we fit into the administration's pedagogical and financial puzzles if we were going to stay with the schools and work with students. The same creative approach can ensure that SEL sticks around even when it is challenged.

A second potential cost of maintaining the status quo is that a lack of intentional planning and support for teachers can render SEL as an "extra thing" that seems out of reach. To begin with, teachers have a lot of responsibilities and not a lot of time. Everything is time-sensitive in a classroom. New programs focused on SEL or the arts have to flow seamlessly into the cross-curricular classroom environment. Teachers want to do a great job for their students, but we must do our part to make it easier for them. Programs have to be relevant to what is happening day-to-day in the classroom and need to fit with everything else teachers have planned.

A third point to consider is the importance of meeting people where they are. To get all students engaged, we need to take our resources and funnel them into something fresh, relevant, and timely. A "one-hit wonder" program with no relevance or sustained effort is not going to help a young child in the urban core of Cincinnati who's wondering where his next meal is coming from or if he's going to be homeless in the next week. We can't just do it the way we've always done it. We must think of all kids and their needs and design programs to reach them.

III. Forecast for the Future

As I mentioned earlier, I first started trying social-emotional practices long before understanding that they fell under a broad concept called SEL. It's interesting to find myself utilizing tools that I had no idea were defined by name until somebody pointed it out to me, comparing my intuition and skill to already-existing research. It was eye-opening to realize that there was an entire country out there trying to figure out the same things while I was plugging away independently.

As discussion around SEL has increased in volume, I'm sure more and more people have had the same experience. There must have been individuals and groups all over working in isolation, not knowing how many others were trying the same things. Now with more connection and conversation around SEL issues and programs to make it happen, the future looks positive. Those who have implemented SEL for a long time now have more opportunities to refine their approach, and those who are just getting started have many more resources and expansive growing support.

We recently had a talk with a large healthcare company about building a program dealing with men's health issues and building resilience for African-American boys. Our first reaction was "The light has come on. Someone is finally paying attention. Let's do it!" We are confident because we already know how to do it. Now the general awareness and support are there to accelerate existing efforts.

IV. Pathway to Success

My solution always starts in one place: getting down on the floor and talking to students at their level. And I mean literally getting down on the floor. We're going to get dirty, but that's what we've got to do. I can't tell you how many times I've said that to colleagues, and I don't mince my words. The difference between what we do in Cincinnati and what everybody else seems to be doing is that I'm going to get down on the floor and talk to kids where they are and not worry about my own personal comfort. I'll get down on the floor with the kids if that's what it takes because, if you do it one time and show someone how you're doing it, you're modeling for the next person. Modeling behaviors is extremely powerful. Demonstrating that you're willing to do whatever it takes makes all the difference to kids. Kids can see how much you care when you're willing to stretch yourself to meet them in their world.

Once we start thinking like that, no one will be able to deter us because the results will make it obvious. We don't need to condescend to colleagues who show resistance or seem lost in implementing SEL. If they don't know what they're doing or feel that they don't, they need to hear good advice from someone. If we're the one in position to share that advice, let's not make them feel foolish. Instead, let's show them the potential. On the flip side, we can't walk in the room assuming people don't know anything about SEL best practices. We must enter knowing that we want to share some information with them and that's all. We must leave the preconceptions at the door, pour our hearts into it, and show how it's done. That's the only way we need to look at it to have a successful conversation.

A major key to success when working with teachers on implementing SEL programs, or really any new initiative, is an awareness of what the teacher goes through and what they deal with in all facets of their job. Understanding what they have to deal with and *being aware* that you need to understand are two different things, and the distinction between them is crucial. The awareness factor helps you relate to individual teachers' needs. For some teachers, everything has to be fulfilled in a portfolio, and they have to make sure to fill out the box and check the square. Others need an extra push to buy in or need more assistance in seeing how to make SEL an intentional part of the day-to-day experience. If teachers aren't entirely on board, social-emotional learning will be dead on arrival.

If we're going to give teachers the opportunity to play in SEL, we must make sure they have the permission to add their own flavor to what they're doing in the classroom. If we tell them that we have a program that will give them ideas and examples where they can use their creativity to "spice up" their lessons, most will be eager to try it. Teachers' unique ingenuity and expertise combined with the right support can make SEL flourish.

So the questions become "What kind of support helps SEL work, and how do we integrate it?" I answer these questions through the lens of the work I've done, in which SEL is combined with literacy programs. The primary goal is getting kids to read. To do so, we need to make the child want to read that book. It must come alive. This same concept can be applied to any subject: math, science, social studies, physical education, world languages, or whatever else. Getting SEL right can get kids engaged and push academics forward.

I believe that including the arts in education is a natural integration of SEL. It makes kids want to learn and helps them find a way in which they best engage with content. The arts allow us to play out an emotion in a safe space. They allow us to play it out in many directions where we wouldn't normally feel inclined to circulate feelings. Art allows us to be who we are and strengthens the common bond that makes us human. When we take that common bond and build wonderful things with it, the rest is gravy.

A great example is a program we worked on to address bullying. During the program, we talked to the students about impressions and their lasting effect. We brought feelings and emotions front and center. Until recently, we typically didn't see many books with lessons on bullying, but with so much violence and terror in our schools taking place in recent years, they are more prevalent. In our program, we used a book called *Chrysanthemum*, in which the main character is a mouse named Chrysanthemum who is teased repeatedly about her name.[2]

Using the book as a script, we presented a live performance. To illustrate the lesson for the kids we used a "wrinkled heart" exercise. The kids created paper hearts and wrote the following poem on them: "Before you speak, be kind and smart. It's hard to heal a wrinkled heart." We told them, "As you listen to the play, anytime you hear something negative about Chrysanthemum, about her name or about her, wrinkle your heart in your hand a little bit. Scrunch it up a little." At the end of the theater performance, we told them to look at their hearts and smooth them out anyway they could, as best they could.

What they found is that it's impossible to get all the wrinkles out. This was a powerful illustration of the impression left by bullying behavior. When we've been treated poorly, we get some of it out over time, but the impression is always there. The image of the wrinkled heart can apply just as much to any emotional trauma children have experienced, not only the trauma from being bullied.

Using literacy as a delivery vehicle for social-emotional content is equally powerful, and perhaps even more so, when families are engaged together. Hosting family literacy nights in a school, where parents join their kids for reading and activities, is a great start. After everyone has read the book together, there are additional lessons and activities throughout the evening. One is to make a craft based on the story. During the craft activity, we project conversation starters onto the wall guiding parents on beginning to talk with their kids. Conversations help to build a trusting relationship, and this activity addresses the challenge of closing the "word gap" for parent and child. Bringing many different parents and children into the room together to find common ground and engage in conversation is a great foundation for addressing social-emotional needs.

I believe success is an emotion, and I know that connecting people with their emotions is necessary when creating an authentic experience. They will take it to heart. We know that everyone wants to feel success, so we create an environment where kids and parents can quickly make progress together. Quick wins may start out small, but they create a feeling that people want to hang onto. Hanging onto that emotion and developing it further is a recipe for sustained, improved relationships.

These are not complex conversations, by the way. But they are positive interactions that start from a place other than "Sit down" or "Be quiet." It's all about the simple concept of allowing the time and space to interact and work on something together in a relaxed environment away from outside stressors.

As you watch families working together, you're witnessing their relationships grow in real time.

Not only do we find ourselves working with all types of families, but we also frequently find ourselves working with children who are experiencing homelessness. For these children, SEL can mean so much, and many teachers probably have students facing this insecurity and don't even realize it. It's not always obvious, but we've seen it enough in our community to know that this is a real issue affecting many kids and families. When we give these kids resources, attention, and support, it provides a sense of worth.

The formula for SEL success remains simple. It's a matter of giving teachers, parents, and other leaders the assurance that they can do it. It's about opening a new door and realizing the social-emotional benefits to be gained. Programs in the performing arts have often said, "A lot of what we do can't necessarily be measured." That is exactly right. We need to be there to see and feel the success happen.

It all comes down to bringing a community together and setting that community into action. Making SEL lasting is all about engagement, dedication, and perseverance. When everyone in education works together and understands the beauty of what each one brings to the equation, we will have great success together.

Editor's Reflection Questions

- Were you doing SEL before you knew it was called SEL, or can you think of another person or program who seemed to be doing this? What were the successes and what were the missed opportunities when the approach wasn't intentional?
- Developing kids into thoughtful members of the community— whether that community is local or global—is one of the objectives of SEL. What are some ways you can expose students to people, cultures, and ideas that they otherwise might miss?
- One of the best ways to gain buy-in for SEL is to make it fun. What are some of your best ideas for making it fun and engaging?

NOTES

1. Read more about No Child Left Behind at *https://www2.ed.gov/nclb/landing.jhtml.*
2. Kevin Henkes. *Chrysanthemum.* (New York: HarperCollins, 1991).

CPSIA information can be obtained
at www.ICGtesting.com
Printed in the USA
LVHW080850300119
605569LV00008B/4/P

9 781501 878008